Edwin Simon

Huslia

Edwin Simon

Huslia

ISBN #0-88839-068-8
Copyright © Yukon-Koyukuk School District 1981
Produced by: Yukon-Koyukuk School District of Alaska
Superintendent: Joe Cooper
Assistant Superintendent-Instruction: Fred Lau
Project Coordinator: Don Kratzer
Editing and Interviews by:
Curt Madison
Yvonne Yarber

Photographs by: Curt Madison (unless otherwise noted)
Materials collected during June of 1978 at Huslia, Alaska
Project funded by the following sources:
Indian Education Grant #553A and #0576
Johnson-O'Malley Grant #EOC 1420-1834
and #EOC 1420-2062

No part of this book may be reproduced by any means without written permission by the publisher.

Published by:
HANCOCK HOUSE PUBLISHERS
1431 Harrison Avenue, Blaine, WA, U.S.A. 98230
HANCOCK HOUSE PUBLISHERS LTD.
19313 Zero Avenue, Surrey, B.C., Canada V3S 5J9

Regional School Board 1981:
Don Honea, Sr. - Chairman
Wally Carlo - Vice-Chairman
Ivan Sipary - Treasurer
Vera Strack - Secretary/Clerk
Alfred Attla, Sr.
Eddie Bergman
William Dayton
Pat McCarty
Eleanor Sweetsir

Printed in Canada

Cataloging in Publication Data

Simon, Edwin.
  Edwin Simon

(Alaska series)
ISBN 0-88839-068-8

1. Simon, Edwin. 2. Koyukon Athabaskan - Alaska - Biography - Juvenile Literature. I Title. II. Series.
E99.E7S54 j970.004'97 C80-091249-7

Cover: Edwin Simon and Galee outside the house in Huslia, June 1979.
Title Page: Front: Beverly Simon, Eliza DeWilde, Sharon Yatlin, Allen DeWilde, Vaughn DeWilde, Al Yatlin Jr., Laona DeWilde, Ray DeWilde.
Middle: Franklin Simon, Lillian Simon, Lee DeWilde, Christopher Simon, Tyson DeWilde, Doreen Simon, Angie Yatlin, Edwin Simon, Tanya Yatlin, Tracy Derendoff, Amilia DeWilde, Lloyd DeWilde.
Back: Eileen Simon, Reba DeWilde, Victor DeWilde, Calvin Simon, Lydia Simon, Eleanor Yatlin, Gladys Derendoff, Huslia 1978.

A Note From A Linguist

As you read through this autobiography you will notice a style and a diction you may not have seen before in print. This is because it is an oral, storytelling style. This autobiography has been compiled from many hours of taped interviews. As you read you should listen for the sound of the spoken voice. While it has not been possible to show all the rhythms and nuances of the speaker's voice, much of the original style has been kept. If possible you should read aloud and use your knowledge of the way the old people speak to recapture the style of the original.

This autobiography has been written in the original style for three reasons. First, the original style is a kind of dramatic poetry that depends on pacing, succinctness, and semantic indirectness for its narrative impact. The original diction is part and parcel of its message and the editors have kept that diction out of a deep respect for the person represented in this autobiography.

The second reason for keeping the original diction is that it gives a good example of some of the varied richness of the English language. English as it is spoken in many parts of the world and by many different people varies in style and the editors feel that it is important for you as a reader to know, understand and respect the wide resources of this variation in English.

The third reason for writing in the original style is that this style will be familiar to many of you who will read this book. The editors hope that you will enjoy reading something in a style that you may never have seen written before even though you have heard it spoken many times.

Ron Scollon
Alaska Native Language Center
University of Alaska
Fairbanks
July 1979

Acknowledgments

This book could not have been produced without the help and encouragement of many people. Lydia Simon, Edwin's wife, gave much of her time, stories, and home, as did Franklin and Lillian Simon. All three of them helped read over the rough draft of the manuscript in Huslia, March 1981. Catherine and Stephen Attla give everyone inspiration, and we were lucky enough to have a little rub off. Madeline Bifelt and Selina Sam provided significant information for the family tree. Eliza Jones of the Alaska Native Language Center continues to supply valuable advice, translations, and notes. Thanks to Ron Scollon for his *Note from a linguist.* Bea Hagen and Cheryl Dehart, both of Manley Hot Springs, shared the typing. Janis Carney and Liza Vernet volunteered proofreading time. The Community School Committee of Manley Hot Springs provides the work space.

From the District Office in Nenana, Bob Maguire survives as the original instigator of the project, while Don Kratzer has taken over as Coordinator. Joe Cooper, Superintendent; Fred Lau, Assistant-Superintendent for Instruction; and Mavis Brown, Administrative Secretary, guided us through the labyrinth of administrative detail. Last, much thanks to the Yukon-Koyukuk School District Regional Board, who continue to support local curriculum.

All royalties from the sale of this book go to the Yukon-Koyukuk School District for the production of more biographies.

This is the first printing of this book. Please notify us of any errors so they can be corrected in future printings.

Foreword

Edwin Simon—Huslia is the eighth in a series of autobiographies of people who live in the eleven villages serviced by the Yukon-Koyukuk School District. These books are designed for upper level elementary students living in rural Alaska although they may well captivate readers of any age.

Most school materials in Alaska come from Outside and mention Alaska peripherally, if at all. We need not be described as a "barren wasteland" on the periphery of the real world. We are a homeland, and the center of a rich and varied but, unfortunately, neglected culture. We hope to bring home a relevant curriculum through this series.

This story of Edwin Simon offers students the opportunity to study some of the changes that have taken place close to home in a short span of time. It is written in six chapters to allow easy breaking points for discussion and activities. Suggested student activities for this book are available from the Yukon-Koyukuk School District office, Nenana, Alaska 99760.

This book is by no means a definitive work. It should be viewed as one part of a much larger picture, a beginning point for teachers in classrooms throughout the Interior.

> Yvonne Yarber
> Curt Madison
> Manley Hot Springs, Alaska
> April 1981

Table of Contents

A Note From A Linguist	5
Acknowledgements	6
Foreword	7
Maps	10
Introduction	11
Glossary	12

CHAPTER ONE — FIRST LIFE

Always Moving Around	14
People Die That Summer	17
White People Start to Come	19
New Names, New Mission	20
Horse Not *Sis*	23
Old Enough to Learn	26
Bear, the Big Chief Stole the Sun	28
Old Man Simon	30
Julia Simon	32

CHAPTER TWO — LIVING IN THE WOODS

First Wife, Margarite	34
Always Help Each Other	37
Medicine People	39
Married to Lydia	40
Sam Dubin	41
Dominic Vernetti	43
Never Bragg	44
KK'ulk'eeyaggazee	46
Wind Is His Boss	46
First Moose	48
No Moose Around Here	50
Through the Ice	52
Fish	55
Teach Her How to Shoot	57

CHAPTER THREE — LYDIA

My First Parents	59
Daddy Had Two Stores	66
Grandma Madeline's First Bread	71
Grandma Julia and Old Man Simon's New Tent	73
All Circle, Hand, Hand, Circle	74
Bear in Hole	75
Bird and Animal Songs	77
Wolverine Songs	78

CHAPTER FOUR — WORK

- River Boat — 80
- Six Years in Dredge — 81
- Huslia Community Store — 83
- Firefighting — 85
- Alaskaland Tourists — 87
- Bilingual and Survival School — 89
- Old Age Pension — 93

CHAPTER FIVE — *NIK'INLA'AN*

- Somebody Shoot — 94
- Stay with Woodsman — 99

CHAPTER SIX — ALL MY LIFE I SPEAK OUT

- Tanana Chiefs — 101
- Talk for Ourselves — 103
- Equal Rights — 105
- Fifty-Dollar Fine — 107
- Advise Doctors — 110
- Speak for the Whole Group — 111
- Cutoff to Huslia — 112

- Post Note — 117
- Appendix A — 118
- Appendix B — 118
- INDEX — 120

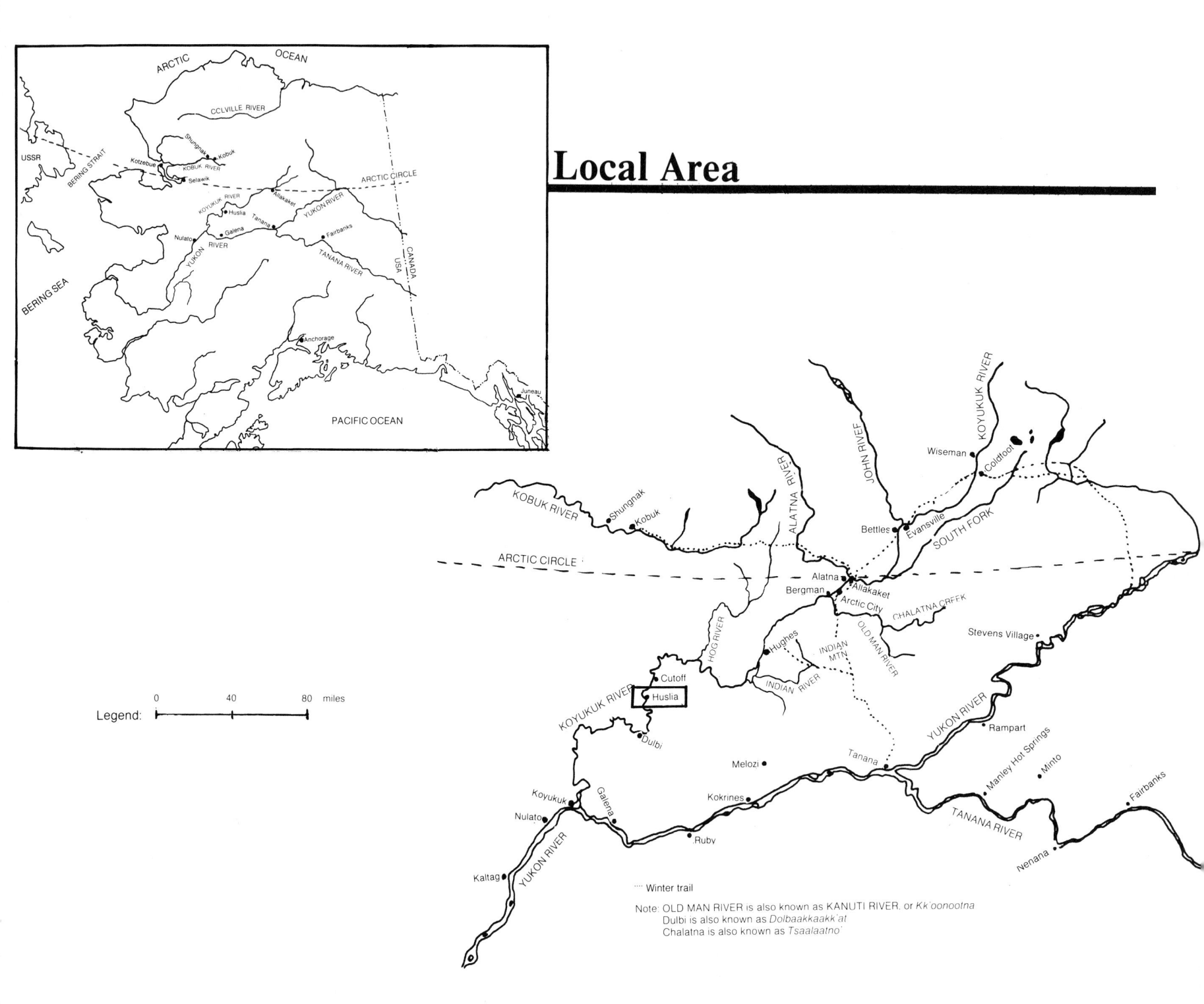

Introduction

Huslia is a Koyukon Athabaskan village located about 220 miles upriver from the mouth of the Koyukuk River. Before 1952 most of the people of Huslia lived sixteen miles upriver at Cutoff. Edwin Simon was a key person in the decision to move the village, as he was a key person in many political activities affecting Indian people. When he died in March 1979, the people of the Interior lost a leader. His notions of fairness and justice crossed all lines of age and race. And he never hesitated to speak out.

Whether he was riding a three-wheel Honda motorcycle in the village, a sno-go on his trapline, or singing a traditional potlatch song, change would not stop him from keeping his Indian nationality. The interviews for this book were done in June 1978 and represent only a few of the stories Edwin liked to tell. Those readers who knew him well will remember many more.

Glossary

Allakaket—An Athabaskan village on the Koyukuk River just north of the Arctic Circle. Its population is about 160. Facilities include a community hall, an airstrip, a post office, a school, and a community office that houses the village phone. These facilities are shared with the thirty or so residents of Alatna, an Eskimo village located across the Koyukuk River. There are no roads to Allakaket, and transportation in the winter is by airplane, snow machine or dogteam. In the summer, travel is by boat or airplane. Electricity is provided by a small generator, and a hand pump village well is on the bank of the river for summer use.

Arctic City—One of the largest Koyukuk River villages, located twelve miles downriver from Allakaket, also known as Moses Village. In 1906 all the people moved to the Episcopal St. John's of the Wilderness mission established at Allakaket.

chicken— Birds of the grouse family such as ptarmigan and spruce grouse.

Cutoff—A Koyukon Athabaskan village on the Koyukuk River, which usually flooded in the spring. The population moved to higher ground in the early fifties and established a village named Huslia after a nearby river.

Dulbi—Once a settlement at the mouth of the Dulbi River. The Koyukon place name as given by Eliza Jones is *Dolbaakaakk'at*, meaning "mouth of the Dolbaatno" or "Dulbi River."

glizzard—Covered with ice. This word is Edwin's invention, probably derived from the words glacier and blizzard.

graft—Taking advantage of one's position to gain illicit profit from government business.

hʉłkanee—Taboo, bad luck sign. (Eliza Jones).

Huslia—Koyukon Indian village on the Koyukuk River established in the early fifties by people from Cutoff. Huslia's present population of about 200 has a public school, an airport, a post office, community center, telephone, television, electricity, and the Native Corporation, *K'oyitł'ots'ina*, a merger of Alatna, Allakaket, Hughes, and Huslia.

Koyukon—Language of the Central Yukon and Koyukuk River Athabaskans.

snaa—Koyukon word for "my child." (Eliza Jones). See Appendix A.

sodaa'—A word used in calling meaning "my older sister." (Eliza Jones). See Appendix A.

Please note: Many Koyukon words and phrases appear throughout the book. They are translated in parentheses by Eliza Jones, whose initials are shown. See Appendix A and B for more Koyukon translations and kinship terms.

CHAPTER ONE — First Life

Always Moving Around

I'm Edwin Simon of Huslia. I was born in 1898, first of October, on Yukon River at Rampart. My folks used to move around long ago. People used to move around long ago. I lived lot of places. Mouth of Old Man, Arctic City, till 1909, then Allakaket till about 1931. After that I live in old Cutoff and last, where I stay now, Huslia.

You look at how old I am and I can tell you I lived three different lives. Like my life now is with electricity, sno-go, airplanes, refrigerator, freezer, radio, even running water. We start to have everything after around 1960. I even have three-wheel Honda to get around.

Second life, before all that stuff, say 1930 to 1960, we have inboard motor and gas boat. That really changed life around here. Start to have gasoline, oil lamp.

My first life is the way my folks used to live. We lived different kind of life altogether. You see, we had no kind of power. Only candle for light. We use birchbark canoe for all that travel. Make poling boat and let dogs tow the boat for us in summer while we pole or paddle upriver. Take our time. We make it though. Like I say, people used to move around long ago. They go where there's game.

My folks used to live around this country here. That's when they used to have muzzle-loader, slow hunting gun. When they start to have .44 long barrel rifle that hold fifteen shells they move away.

There was no moose, no caribou around here so they go where there's game. About 1894, people start to move up Old Man River where

Edwin Simon.

there's lots of caribou and lots of moose. Summertime they go up head of river, hunt sheep. There's lots of game up there when they got rifle. I used to hunt sheep with Oscar Nictune way up Koyukuk River, Alatna River. Stay out two, three months.

They all located in mouth of Old Man River about fifteen miles below Allakaket. Lot of fish where the Old Man River comes out there. My mother and my father build fish trap. That's the kind of place people used to look for long ago, where there's lots of fish and lots of game. Not much White people around yet, at that time.

Well, in the winter of 1897-98, the whole group of people went out hunting. That's what they used to do. And they keep traveling toward Rampart, toward the Yukon River. Mom used to tell us all these things that happen before I was born. Funny question I ask her one time. I say, "Mom, what you people do with your things? Where you people put your stuff when you travel like that, hunting all winter?"

"What stuff?" she say. "We ain't got nothing. Either got muzzle-loader or rifle, bow and arrow, and one axe. We got nothing. So, we don't leave nothing behind."

Well, I come to myself and I say, "That's a foolish question I ask Mom because they sure didn't have nothing, they just keep moving."

Make igloo house everywhere. They dig about four feet underground. Make the house half in and half out of the ground.

They got ax to cut poles and sod. That's how they make house. I seen one. They make tunnel to get in. That's what they do.

So this winter, 1897-98, whole group of Indians, my folks, could be six or seven family, keep traveling toward Rampart. Lot of snow. Moose couldn't walk. So they just kill moose and caribou. Get their food easy. Then they came to Steven's Village not far from Yukon.

Lydia and Edwin Simon Collection

Edwin Simon and Oscar Nicture beaver trapping near Huslia 1962.

Snow starting to melt so whole group of Indians spring in with Steven's Village people.

My mother say, lots of water that spring. They drift down to Rampart. Camp on the hill when they get there. Flood. They see lots of cabins going down. That's the highest water they ever known.

Eighteen ninety-eight, highest water.

Rampart was big village at that time. One of the biggest. Lot of people, Indian, White. Army in there too. Army camp with soldiers stationed there. My folks and the whole group of Indians from Koyukuk River made a little village across from Rampart on our side, on this side of the Yukon. They had log cabins.

They stayed there that year. My mother told me I was born in the fall. October 1898. Few months after that was the first time they seen New Year. All those Rampart people celebrate. People holler New Year and Christmas and everything. New Year, 1899.

Eighteen ninety-nine, they left Rampart. Back for Koyukuk.

Mother say the days are getting longer. I was just few months old when they leave. She say all the bath I got is they threw me in the snow. They used to roll us in the snow in the morning so we live long time and be tough.

When they get close to the head of Old Man my mother say they stay out in the mountain too long. They didn't look at no calendar. When

Michael Simon in his otter tail parka.

Ludi Hope, Alfred Isaac's sister in Allakaket 1932.

they start down to head of Old Man on the flats, no more snow. They have to throw all the sleds away and start to pack. Pack clothes, cooking stuff, everything to where they're going to spring.

Everybody start to work at canoe. Every spring they do that. Everywhere they go they make birchbark canoe. When they finish they come down mouth of Old Man and located in there. You see, people never had a village long ago, around here. Maybe one family stay here, another family in there. Always moving around. Only time they all get together is when they had potlatch.

Down Dulbi used to be big village. Lots of igloos. But not around here. Maybe couple igloos in one place. *Dolbaakaakk'at* was the old village down there. Where Red Shirt medicine man used to stay. They don't stay in one village like we do right now.

"People Die That Summer"

There was a lot of people in 1902. I remember part of it. People died that summer. I was four years old. Sternwheeler steamboat came up with the measles. Sternwheeler carrying all those White people. Prospectors, gold mining people. Went all around Yukon and way up to Bettles. All the way up and all the way down people died.

They had a name for it. *K'inaalnonh di saanh,* they say. That's the name of "People Die That Summer." That's the only name I hear. Afterward when I get to be man I ask White people, "What kind of sickness?" They say it was measles. I never get measles.

How we never got sick is, about July, my mother and father go up Old Man River. Up about fifteen miles from the mouth to this place called Lynx Creek. We stay there and put fish trap in again. We

Steamer Nenana going up Nine Mile Slough Koyukuk River 1949.

never see nobody.

Pretty soon it start getting dark again. Days getting shorter. My father said,"I'm going down to Koyukuk River, visit people." He was gone one night and come back. He say, "Lot of people died. Some whole families just wipe out. Kids, old people. Everybody die." That measle is what wipe out all our people. We never had no sickness again till 1934, 1935. Well, 1918 we got a touch of big flu. Before you people was born. Lot of people die all over the world. And then, quarantine all over too. We never get that flu up to Allakaket. In old Cutoff village we got touch of it but nobody died. Measles is what killed a lot of people and TB. People never had TB or measles here before White people come.

Around 1935 we had measles up here again. Lot of people died. We lost twelve people up Cutoff. All my family was sick. We lost one baby. We close the windows and everything, stay in the house. I understand about how measles is.

I never got sick. I was the one make coffin. I handle lots of dead people. Bury people, bring people down with inboard gasboat. I don't know why I didn't get sick. Then I say, "Well, I work for the fellow that kill us. I was hired to make coffin and handle dead people. I don't think I'll get sick."

My father used to say, "White people never got sick. That's their sickness. They come from Outside with it. That's theirs and they wouldn't get sick with it. When any kind of sickness first come to Alaska we Native people die with it. Because we're not used to it." He was right.

Lydia and Edwin Simon Collection

George Jimmy, Rebecca Jimmy, Inyas 1922.

White People Start to Come

White people start to come up the river before I remember good. In 1898, there's lots of White people starting to go all over. But they don't bother Indians. There's only one man we know get killed on this river. That's John Bremner. Old man. Prospector down Dulbi. Young fellow kill him.

Well, this old medicine man they called Old Man Bob. He adopt this kid. His nephew, his sister's boy. I don't know what this boy's name. He and Old Man Bob stay down mouth of Dulbi. Here is White man going down and this old man say to his nephew, "You always steal tobacco from me. Why don't you go down and kill that White man for tobacco."

So this young fellow, maybe sixteen years old followed the White prospector down with canoe. Pretty soon that John Bremner stop and have a fire. That young fellow shot him with muzzle loader. People find out and take this young fellow down to mouth of Koyukuk and hang him there. Just the young boy. Not the old man. Old man come back with canoe and it's his fault.

That's only story I know about killing around here. White people help us and we help White people. I remember I had blood poisoning when I was about eighteen years old. Me and my brother was out head of Old Man. I cut my foot. Oh, I was suffer. Cut it with little ax. Never take care of it. No medicine. All my skin came off.

My brother was out and he come to White trapper by the name of Henry Parker. Lone White man about fifty years old. Trapping. My brother come back to me and say, "I come to a White man. I told him about you. He say he want you over there."

So they haul me to that White man. He had a little bottle, black stuff. Carbolic acid I guess thay call it. It kill poison. He say he bought that when he left Seattle for five dollars. He say, "It takes poison to kill poison." It just look like iodine, but it's not iodine. It's poison.

He put ten drops in wash basin, hot water, and he soak my leg. Three days my skin start to grow. Take care of my leg. Four or five days I start to walk. If we never come to that fellow I might have lost my leg. Well White people help us and we help them. All over. Bettles, Arctic City, Hughes. Indians and White people never have trouble. Always help each other. Always. I think of that old Henry Parker. Save my leg.

New Names, New Mission

Nineteen six, that's when I remember pretty good. I'm seven or eight years old. They had an Indian village in Arctic City about ten or twelve miles below Allakaket. In February me and Mom was out snaring rabbits. Make a fence for rabbits and make snare. It's cold weather.

Those days used to be cold weather, fifty or sixty below. I remember because in 1930, my father say, "Cold get old. No more cold weather. Long ago dog tail freeze so they keep dogs in igloo tunnel." So I remember when I'm seven years old it's cold.

Well, in winter of 1906, Archdeacon Stuck came. That's first preacher that ever come to Koyukuk River. Came with dogteam. He had an interpreter with him from Tanana. Fellow by the name Dick White. Hudson Stuck start to preach and start to baptize people. There was about nine houses at Arctic City and he use one of the biggest house and preach every night with interpreter.

Some of us here already baptize before he came along. My father

John Nelson in Koyukuk 1908.

went to Tanana to be baptized. My mother say I was baptized in Rampart after I was born by Mr. Privitch, Episcopal Church. But Archdeacon Stuck baptize people that never was baptized. He give them new names.

I have to laugh though. You know all us people can't speak English. And White people that came up them days give all kinds of name to Indians. And when Archdeacon Stuck start to baptize people he say, "What your name?" Well, this interpreter, sometime he smile. People answer back all kinds of name. Sometime dirty words White people gave Native.

When it's dirty word or crazy name that man or woman answer, Archdeacon just smile, open his Bible and give them new name. Ned, Thomas, Tommy, William, he give them new English name. I already had my name Edwin. All my family had Athabaskan name except me. I just had one name, that's all.

So every night Archdeacon Stuck preach to the people. One mistake he made is he want to take pictures. It's nighttime. They're all in this one big house with coal oil lamp. One little lamp. Archdeacon Stuck put his big camera on tripod by the door. Big camera and light have to be out.

Well, he blew the light out and told everybody to stand up. You ought to hear them people start to talk. Especially old people. They say in their language, "What you do? What you blow the light out for?" Everybody get scared.

Then, pretty soon, POOOooshshhhhhhhhhhhhhh!. Big light flash!. Everybody holler. First the tripod go one side and the preacher fall to other side. Everybody rush out. Go home.

Next day, church again. My father say, "No, don't go." They got scared. Everybody got scared. They don't know that's light for

Mrs. Bizook in Koyukuk 1918.

Little Jimmy, Martha, George Jimmy in Ruby 1917.

picture. They don't know what's picture. I guess he try to explain. Few people went back to church.

That was 1906. Archdeacon travel back and forth. He went mostly to Arctic City village and up Alatna. There was only about three or four cabin up Allakaket on Alatna side, Eskimo side.

Archdeacon Stuck say he wants to make Mission at Allakaket where the two rivers come together. Mostly he talk to people at Arctic City but part of the people was against it. People located at Arctic City on account of Old Man River. Lot of fish and game there. They don't want to move.

Part of the people was for it. He told them, there's lot of Eskimo up Alatna River. So he want to put the Mission where the Alatna and Koyukuk Rivers meet. Build the Mission for Eskimo and Indian. Well, he was right too. There was lot of Eskimo people up Alatna. But there was bigger village at Arctic City. Good ground, better ground.

Summer of 1907, they build a Mission up Allakaket, St. John's of the Wilderness. That's what killed the Arctic City village. Some of the people from Arctic City moved to Allakaket. About the same time or maybe short time afterward, my uncle discovered gold at Indian Creek, back of Hughes. That's what start Hughes. Rest of the people from Arctic City moved there.

My uncle, Alfred Isaac, he's the fellow that discovered the gold. Him and my older brother Andrew spend whole summer in Indian Mountain. Go up, go down creeks. Go way up Indian River. Spend whole summer to find that prospect. They call the place Indian Creek and Indian Mountain because this Indian discovered the gold.

But you see, they got no sense enough to hold ground. My uncle sold his claim for a thousand dollars. He got that much out of his find. My brother never got nothing out of it. He stake ground and

Lydia and Edwin Simon Collection

Sam Hope, Ludi Hope and an adopted Japanese boy.

some White people jump that ground. What they call claim jumpers, they just take ax and cut a person's name off and write their own name.

I'll tell you something. I been all over. Head of John River, head of Wild River, all over. And I used to work at mining camp sluicing, dredge. Mostly that's what I used to work. A lot of people ask me why I don't prospect.

I tell them, "I don't buy gold pan or shovel. Never. I don't take them when I was hunting. No place." I say, "No use. If I find gold I'm going to find it for somebody. That's what my brother and uncle do. They just find gold for somebody."

Horses not *Sis*

In 1908 my folks went up the Old Man River. Three family went up in the summer. They plan to winter up there. Trap. It was Old Paul and my Auntie Lucy Paul, that's Lavine Williams' in Hughes mother and stepfather. Other family was my brother-in-law Ned and sister Lily, my father's daughter from his first wife. She got only one son now up there in Allakaket, Simon Ned. So three family went up Old Man River.

In September we got up there to Birch Creek, Birch River. Way up. People kill lot of moose off so not many moose. There, we see moose track around. Pretty soon my brother-in-law Ned say, "No." He say in Indian, "That's horses. They got shoes on. Haw, two!" So everybody look at it and that's right.

Pretty soon it got to be fall so my father and the other man go out and hunt bear in their den. It's just about freezing time. That's what people used to do all the time. I was staying home with my mother. My mother say, "We're going to move down to another creek where there's good place for fishing." Whitefish Creek, about four miles down. Put up tent.

Those women say they'll go up the cache and get little flour and sugar. They tell me and Aunty Lucy's little girl to stay in tent. Don't go out they tell me. I was about ten years old, little girl is younger than me. They go across creek with birchbark canoe. Go up cache. That cache is at place they stay about a week ago. And while they're up in cache a White man come to them. He's lost. He got nothing. No gun.

Pretty soon I hear them coming. I look out the tent. There's three of them! Here's a White man with them. They come inside and I see he's small. He looks pretty good.

He start to talk. His name is Mike. He say, "I kill my two horses this fall." That's just what he said. I'm ten years old. I know what is horses. But my mother, she tell her older sister, cousin, "*Sodaa,* your husband killed two bear. This White man seen them hunters."

I know what happen right there. She think he say, "Paul killing two *sis.*" *Sis* is bear you know. Our language. I tell her this Mike say "This fall" not "Paul." And "horses" not "*sis.*" White man can't say *sis*. I tell my mother, "You know them big animal pull the boat, pull the house last summer in Arctic City. That's horses moved the house back. I seen them."

"Oh no, you don't know what you talk about," she tell me. So I don't say nothing. But I know it's horses this guy Mike killed. When my father and Paul come back they can't understand this guy themselves. Can't understand English.

Pretty soon my brother-in-law Ned and my sister came back to us from where they camp just before freeze-up. Ned can talk to this guy. Mike tell him that he got lost and killed his two horses this fall. That's

Photo by Clemons, circa 1910.

all he live on. He left Tanana in June to Bettles. He's taking horses so they can haul freight from Bettles to Wiseman or Coldfoot. You see, they used to take two horses to pull one scow, barge with freight. Sometimes big scow take four horses to pull. Line up river you see.

Well, this fellow got lost from Tanana. He go up head of Old Man fool around there all summer. He kill his horses for meat and make raft there someplace. He swamp too, lost his gun. He was long ways from Koyukuk River. If my folks never go up and find him he would freeze.

Well, he stay with us about two weeks during freeze-up. During that time I watch him. He sleep in one of them tents with us. Every night I see him put his hand across his mouth slow and then take it away. I watch him. And in the morning he do the same way. I tell my father and he say, "Oh, he killed them horses this summer and that's horses guts he eat. He got dry horses guts in his pocket. That's what he eat." But I didn't believe it. I know there's something.

Then, come to find out afterward, when he get back to Bettles he talk to his own people. He don't want to show us his false teeth because people might get scared of him. That's why he never tell us. He has false teeth you see!

After freeze-up my mother give him moccasin. Moose skin moccasin. My Aunty Lucy give him moose skin mittens. Everybody tell him it's about fifty miles to Allakaket. They tell him to go that way. I think my father worry about him. My father think he would never make it. Next day my father start to follow him. Find out he's going east instead of west. Go back up to where he been all summer.

My father come back that night. He start to talk. He say, "We seen this White man. What we're going to say to him? He can't make it alone. He's going up to head of Chalatna again." That river goes into Old Man, Chalatna they call it. "He don't go toward Allakaket. He's going to freeze this time. Somebody might think we kill him or something because we seen that man first. You people have to go after him. Take him to people down Allakaket or someplace."

Next morning, my brother-in-law Ned and our older brother Andrew pack up and follow him. They take him to Allakaket. No pay, nothing. Fifty miles, hundred miles round trip. They walk, lead him. About twelve mile before they get to Allakaket this Mike is played out. So one of them stay with him there and one go to the village. Tell them, "We find a White man and he's played out up there." People help him.

From there he stay at Bettles. Next year April, he went back Outside. I seen him pass through there. Mike. I don't know what his last name but first name I know pretty good.

Old Enough to Learn

Well then, in 1909, when we get back to Arctic City, everybody ask me, "What your mamma and your aunty say when White man come to your place?" I tell them the whole thing, what they said. People laugh. My mother come in. She heard I said what she tell her cousin, "Paul killing two *sis*." My mother start to spank me with old broom. I got under the bed. She's mad at me for telling on them and people laugh you know.

Well, that March, first part of March, she say, "You go up Allakaket. Go to school. Go up, stay with your cousin. You know what we say when White man come to us. We can't talk. You go to school now."

I went up with somebody and stay with Bill Bergman's family the first time I go to school. I was eleven years old, 1909. It was all right, the Mission school. We had two teachers. We had Mrs. Burke and interpreter, Celia Wright. That's Gareth Wright's aunty, that dogman in Fairbanks. She come from Tanana, Indian girl. She was real educated woman. Talk our language and interpret for us. This Mrs. Burke talk and Celia Wright tell us what the teacher say. But the biggest part of it is, half or maybe one-quarter of students is Eskimo. Interpreter can't do nothing for Oscar and them boys.

We get summer off from school and then I start again in fall. I finish only first grade. I go to school till I was thirteen years old, 1911. Then my father say, "You're thirteen, you're big boy now. You have to go out and trap with us. You got to learn how to hunt, trap, learn how to make what kind of boat we use, snowshoes and sleigh." He says, "That's for your life. Cause you got to stay here. You got to live here. You aren't going to go no place. You got to make living just the way we do. You're old enough to learn now."

So he took me out of school and I went out packing. Three of us. My father, older brother, and me. Went up Chalatna about thirty miles. Pack. No tent. We stay around there one week. Trapping everything. Lynx, fox, marten, otter. And hungry. If we don't kill rabbit or spruce hen we go without eating.

I just make that first trip with them. We get back to the village. Over a week afterwards my father and brother make another trip up Chalatna, check traps. I stay at home.

Well, then before Christmas my father say, "You boys go back there. Check them trap." Two of us. My older brother. We walk over. My brother was two or three years older than me. Big boy. But he was scared all the time. I wasn't scared. Me, I was thirteen years old.

Lydia and Edwin Simon Collection

Caroline Paul and others from Koyukuk 1940.

Well, coming back to village we camp. He just cry all night. I don't think he even sleep. I say, "what's wrong?"

"I don't think it's going to be daylight" he say. "Long time ago it get dark. That time bear, the big chief stole the sun. It's going to be the same thing. Daylight won't come back."

I don't believe him. I asked him, "Did you sleep?"

"Yeah," he tell me, "and we got no time. It's not going to be light. Let's go."

Still I don't believe him but we travel home. I know winter days get short. But every day there's some light. It wouldn't happen like our old story, I thought, not first time we camp. But he's scared so we walk. About four miles from the village it start to get daylight! Well, that's the first time we camp by ourself you know.

Bear, the Big Chief, Stole the Sun

That story my brother worry about, it's long story. But I'll tell you little bit. The story is, it was dark long ago. They say big shot brown bear stole the sun and moon. All the time dark.

Pretty soon lot of people tell this crow, big medicine man, "*Tseek'aałaa'*, old man, why don't you look for the sun? People can't stay like this in dark all the time. We'll give you lots of grub and stuff. You go look for the sun." So he flew up. Look for bear, big chief that stole the sun.

Well, crow have to do all kind of things to get that sun away from bear. That crow fool people all the time. That's why he's good to get sun back from big chief. At last, when crow get sun from bear he fly with it. He got on big, high tree. He cut it up and threw it up for sun and moons. Twelve moon he name, Indian name.

Like, *Mininh tots'eeyh liyaayee* is May, spring when you put canoe in the water. And pretty soon is *Ggaal nogha'*, king salmon eye, that's the time king salmon come, June. Another one is *Mininh k'idkidlee*, that's when ducks got no feather, or shake their feather, July.

August is *Mininh daak'ilk'ilee*, moose always take the skin off their horns. September I forgot. October is *Mininh diditeeyee*, they call that freeze-up time. And November is *Sooga zo'o'*, marten sun, that's when they start to trap martens.

Anyway, there's twelve different names that crow give when he cut up big sun and threw these. That's how daylight came back.

List of Months

(From *Dinaakkanaaga Ts'inh Huyoza* by Eliza Jones — Junior Dictionary for Central Koyukon Athabaskan)

January	*Mininh neelkk'aa nodzaanh' eelkigee*—Month of the days going from short to long.
	Neelkk'aa nodzaanh dilaayee—One that separates long and short days.
February	*Tilil zo'o'*—Eagle month.
March	*KK'olkk'eey zo'o'*—Month of the hawk.
April	*Hutinhzo'o'*—Month of the spring crust.
May	*Mininh tots'eeyh liyaayee*—Month boats are put in the water.
June	*Ggaalnogha'*—King salmon eye.
	Mininh hudinyaaghee—Month everything grows.
July	*Noolaaghanogha'*—Dog salmon eye.
	Mininh tok'aggoyhk'uhudilaayee—Month ducklings are put in water.
August	*Saanlaaghanogha'*—Silver salmon eye.
	Mininh nok'it'on'didaaghee—Month in which leaves fall.
September	*Noldlaagha nogha'*—Chinook salmon eye.
	Huyts'in'lookk'a nogha'—Falltime fish eye.
October	*Mininh diditeeyee*—Freeze-up month.
	Mininh totl'eetl-'adaghee—Slush-ice-in-river month.
November	*Sooga zo'o'*—Marten month.
December	*Huyh kk'aatl'o la'onee*—End of the year.

Our people got lot of stories. Our old people tell us. They have those stories about long ago. They have story about the flood too.

Only one thing they don't have story about is this big bone animal they find around here, mastodon.

My grandpa, my mother's uncle, was over hundred years old when he died. I ask him if he heard story about it. *Nin'yah k'itł'ina* (mastodon, literally, "underground bones of something" E.J.) they call it. That's the name for that mastodon. I ask them old people. Nothing. They never had no story about it. But above Allakaket there's lot of bones in there. Must be big flock live there long ago.

Old Man Simon

My father was good man. He never argue with nobody. He was good hunter, so he teach us how. Us five brothers. When we all growed up, all of us was good hunters. See, you got to have a good person that raise you. He was honest man. Quiet. My mother was the one used to talk.

Old Man Simon. That's my father. Nobody know how old he was. Must be over ninety when he died in 1937. They say he was white skinned. Taller than me. He's a good six-footer. He's white but he was born before Russian people come. He can't have a White man father.

Three summers a fellow named Doctor Hrdlicka used to come down this Koyukuk River. Look at the Indian People. See what kind of people we are. See where we came from. I used to be interpreter for him in Allakaket when I was young. He test the people. Measure people.

Must be my father's freak. He's white. Blue eyes. Just bald headed. Never had hair. He's just born like that. My sisters used to have blonde hair. But he's Indian. He talk Indian. And he's

Lydia and Edwin Simon Collection

Old Man Simon, Edwin's father. Blonde and blue eyed, he was a well known medicine man.

medicine man. Born up here, what they call Timber Lake. Up above here about fourteen, sixteen miles. That's where they used to live.

There used to be medicine people all over. One in every village. Woman or man. Long ago. Man, woman, same thing. Put something over their head. They go around sing and people sing with them. Something you can't see, talk with them. My father was like that. They got medicine songs.

If there's more than one medicine man in village, they got to get along. But sometime, they're kind of selfish. They want to be the big shot. That's when they have little trouble. But, it's all right.

Well, my father, he say, "No more medicine people in Alaska, after this. All Outside people take that something we make medicine on. *Sinhtaala*. Outside people took the whole thing. They took it away from us." That's what my father say when I move to Cutoff.

There was another big medicine man down Koyukuk Station. Andrew Pilot. His father was the Red Shirt Medicine Man down at Dulbi, *Dolbaakkaakk'at,* long time ago. Well, Andrew Pilot come up here to old Cutoff village. He said the same thing what my father said, "*Sozaa', yoonaan hut'aan sinh taal oołneek. Kkudaa ts'aanok'ahootoł'olaa.*" What he say is, "Outside people take what we made medicine on. Alaska people no more medicine man."

They were right, you see. No more medicine people in Alaska. Like Outside, there's lots of medicine man yet right now. But none in Alaska. I think about that. Same thing two medicine man say.

One time, I must be pretty small, but I was born already. Say about 1901. There was medicine man from South Fork. Big old man. I forget his name. Good man. He's a good hunter and people think a lot of him. He spend his summer on sternwheel boat, *City of Paris*. Go down the Yukon. He's a pilot for them, see.

Well, that medicine man die coming back up this Koyukuk River.

Lydia and Edwin Simon Collection

Funeral in Koyukuk, Tony Patsy, Cecelia Carry, David, Old Mary.

It's September, getting dark. My mother said they buried him where they call "creeks come out beyond the hill" the town of old Bergman's in there. White people too. Mother say we live across there when I was small.

Pretty soon that big sternwheeler *City of Paris* go upriver and people find out that medicine man died and they buried him some other place. Well then, another medicine man, he holler. That's his nephew. He just holler. That night *City of Paris* burned up. All that's left is a pile of that iron and old boilers.

After that, people said the medicine man had steamboat. We used to hear steamboat coming up. Closer, closer, then no more noise. Lot of people round here hear that. In Allakaket, too. We hear, whoosh, whoosh, whoosh, boat coming. People say that South Fork medicine man was pilot. After my father die I said, "Yeah, and my father is the engineer in there."

Steamboats stop coming up quite a while ago. I suppose around 1930. Nineteen twenty-five maybe. Still we'd hear that steamboat. Daytime, nighttime, any time. Funny thing. Well, about ten years, maybe more, we don't hear that.

Julia Simon

My mother was pretty rough. Julia Simon. She's the one that raised us. The one that talked to us boys and girls. If we don't do what she says, better look out! She would go after us. She make us do it.

My mother used to say, "You have to kill something and make good living like other people. If you don't and got bad name, we women cry for you. Just like they say, criminal don't pay. It's going to look back at you." My mother used to say that to us five boys. Andrew, Johnny, me, Frank, and Lee. "*Yuhts'a kk'a nok'ahoonoditoł.*" That means, "If you do some bad things to people. Hurt people. It's going to look back at you the last end. You'll get the worst part of it." That's just like going to school when my mother used to talk.

My folks used to have big log house in Allakaket where we grow up. No rooms but we had beds all around. We had nothing. Just little cookstove and heater. That's all. Them people had nothing in them days. But every one of us have beds.

Well, us brothers not married yet. Young. We can't bring girls in my mother's house. Can't do it. She kick like everything. Tell us, "You not going to marry to that girl. You don't have to bring girls in the home." Oh my. And if girl happens to be over and sit on our blanket she say, "Hey, don't sit on my boy's blanket! No good. *Hutłanee.*" Just like womans can't step over man's clothes, she say something. Bad luck. Man can't kill nothing.

Just like me. I talk to my girls and my boys. Lots of old time ways. I tell them how my mother raised us. How old people raised us for our future. I believe what my mother say. She's big woman. Died in 1945. Could be she was little over eighty-five years old.

CHAPTER TWO — Living in the Woods

First Wife, Margerite

The way we used to get married long ago, they have to look way back. See how the family act. If the other family didn't treat their woman right, the woman family wouldn't let their daughter get married to that man. People know each other all over. Up and down the river. Every village you know what kind of people it is. What kind of man and what kind of woman.

We don't just go get married to who we wanted. Parents decided. That's the old way. The Indian way. Less trouble too. I've been married to Lydia since 1932, over forty-five years. And I was married nine years before that. I was lucky. One of the lucky men never had trouble with women.

I got married the first time in Allakaket. I was twenty-one. There was two or three girls I could get married with, but my mother picked one. She tell me, "This family here is good from way back. They treat their husbands good all the time." So that's the way I got married.

From Allakaket we used to go out sixty or seventy miles trapping with dogs. We never think nothing of it. We never think we work hard. First time when I got married to my wife Margerite, we had only two dogs. Because we couldn't catch much fish. Twenty-one years old and I had nothing. But I was healthy and I worked.

One thing, I should have built my own house the first place. That's what I tell everybody, all the young people. When a man gets married,

Alfred Isaac, Margarite Simon, Julia Simon Allakaket 1919 in a beaded picture frame made by Lydia Simon

he should build his own house. Never live with your folks. That's where the trouble is. If, suppose, my boy get married and live with me in here with his wife. Well, there's always trouble. That's why persons can't get along with each other. They have to go on their own. I learned that.

The first summer I was married I built a house with my father-in-law, Alfred Isaac, my wife's father. I was going to live with him for a while. Then I went up help my own father build new house too. Same summer. Instead I should have built my own house.

That winter I went out trapping. Come back Christmastime. We stay in her father's house, or her mother's house. I couldn't get along. I don't like the way they talk and things like that. So we move out, up to my mother's place. That's the house I built with them too. We move up just during New Year time. Crowd.

We stay in there twenty days. Couldn't get along with my mother. Only two dogs but we got tent and stove and we move out. We went over to where they call Chalatna. About thirty miles from Allakaket, we make camp in there. January. Cold. We stay there rest of the winter, trap. We don't stay with nobody no more.

That spring we haul boat over to head of Old Man and hunt muskrat. I bought one dog so we had three. Pull that rowboat over. We got canoe and hunt muskrat. We got about 350 rats and seven beaver. We came out of Old Man about the fourth of June and went right up to Allakaket. We just stay there one night and went up cut house logs.

Fourth of July I have ridge pole on already. I got big logs to saw. And we can't buy no lumber. We whipsawed everything. Saw that up for floor. Episcopal mission give me one door and two windows.

I had open house in the fall. Little house, 14' x 16'. One

Lydia and Edwin Simon Collection

Ginsus Wholecheese 1920.

storekeeper give me little cookstove for open house. Another store over there give me Coleman lamp, gasoline lamp present. Pretty good.

We stayed there, me and my wife. Nobody boss us. That's why I tell everybody, when you get married, never stay with your wife's mother or father or your husband's father and mother. Never. You got to build your own house. I say two family can't live in one house. They never get along. Especially me, I'm not an easy man to get along with, you know.

I told my son Franklin before he get married, "Build your own house and stay in there." He did. He built that back road and he got two building in there.

Dean Wilson, fur buyer, Frank Simon and unidentified man wolf furs, Huslia 1981.

Always Help Each Other

After I was married to Margerite I trap in mail trail sixty miles from Allakaket to Melozi. There was a lot of traffic them days, lot of traveling between Tanana and Bettles, Wiseman. People traveling. Mail cabins, government cabins every twelve miles, twenty miles, fifteen miles. I used to kill moose and caribou. And I never sold one piece of meat.

White people come to me, I give them meat. Caribou meat, a steak, anything. They ask me. They want to buy it. I say no. Never sell meat in this country. We always help each other.

First part of September we go out in the mountain, hunt beaver, caribou, and bear. Then we make a cache out there. One time we killed fourteen caribou and one brown bear. We make cache just like a house, eight logs high and six feet wide. We put poles across and hang all that meat so it wouldn't spoil. We put poles underneath, poles on top, and a big tree on top so no bear or wolverine get in there. A really good cache.

I had three dogs and I borrow two more. I borrow sleigh and middle November we go out and haul that meat. There was my father, father-in-law, and fellow by the name of Little Beatus. Four dogteam. We got to Big Lake thirty-five miles from here and camp in mail cabin.

In the morning I always stay behind those people to make kindling and shavings. Kind of fix the house up before we leave. That's the rule. You have to leave enough wood for the next person that's going to come. I bring in wood to make kindling and shaving, then I follow them.

Quarter mile away there is another little cabin. I get there and there's White man in there. Old fellow. He must be seventy-five, I figure. Small. He's bent up like that. I talk with him. I don't know who he was. I never even catch his name. He's going from Bettles to Tanana pulling a little hand sleigh. You see people was leaving Wiseman. No more gold. Gold run out. Lot of people going back to Yukon. Year of 1921. Gold is kind of played out. Mining camps and people have to leave.

Well, I talk to him. I tell him, "Hey, you want some meat?"

"Oh," he say, "I got no money."

"You don't have to have money," I tell him. Then I look in the sleigh. Pull out front quarter of caribou, arm. Fat. I give it to him. I say, "It's ninety miles from here to Tanana. That should take you to Tanana. Ninety miles more you got to go."

"Nice young man, thank you," he say.

Then he got no light. I tell him, "Why you have no light?"

"I got no candle," he say.

"I got a lot of candle," I told him.

"Oh," he say, "That's all right. This meat is all I care for."

I went down to Old Man Creek flat and here's my father, father-in-law, and Beatus. They make fire. Making cup of tea. I say, "You people see that White man in that cabin this morning?"

"Yeah, he was standing there," they say. "I talk with him. I give him caribou arm and he was glad. And he got no candles."

Then my father-in-law say, "You know that man before?"

I say no.

"Well, what you do that for?" he say.

Then my father say, "*Snaa*, my boy, maybe he don't look good to you. That's why you did that."

"Yeah," I say, "he got to go ninety miles to Tanana and I feel sorry for him. Maybe he got nothing. He don't even have candle," I tell them.

Medicine People

Lydia's father was medicine man, Francis Olin. Not her mother, but her grandmother and grandfather on her father's side. Olin's father was big medicine man. My father, too, was medicine man. They could tell you things.

Nineteen twenty-eight to twenty-nine we were trapping halfway between Tanana and Allakaket. Johnny Oldman and us, my family. My wife Margerite, adopted daughter, and rest of my family. We wanted to go to Tanana with our fur for the seventeenth of March celebration. My father say, "Don't go. Don't go," he say. "Sickness. You people going to come down with sickness down there." I pretty near back out.

Night before we left he make medicine. He quit around twelve o'clock and he say, "Sit down, smoke. Only one sleigh come back around here on the crust. One of you will stay down there all summer. That's what you go down for." I pretty near back out.

But this Johnny Oldman, "Oh, we got lot of fur," he said. "We got to sell our fur."

Nineteen twenty-nine, that was big flu epidemic in Tanana. We get there, everybody down with flu. Lot of people died. I got down with flu too. Me and my wife. But I had a fellow take care of my dogs. Fellow name of Edgar Kallands. He work at N. C. Store. He's down living at Kaltag now. He take care of my dogs and he come to see me everyday. He's my buddy. Little younger than me but I call him buddy all the time.

Don't go out. I was sick for three days. Awful. And I stay in house one week. Never went out. That's the way with the flu. My wife Margerite was pretty sick too.

Around first of April I start to go back to Allakaket with eleven

Bobby Vent, Wilson Sam, Frank Albert, Francis Olin in Cutoff 1949.

Tanana, N.C. Co. Corbusier Cottage in foreground, circa 1910.

dogs. Started to haul back. We had everything scattered around Melozi where we trap. Tent all over and traps. We got back to Allakaket twenty-seventh of April. Five o'clock in the morning on the crust.

My father and brothers were way up head of Oldman about sixty to seventy miles hunting rats. Rat camp. Edward Bergman was there too. He's married to my older sister Charlotte. He's just like Oscar Nictune, he went to some school and he writes pretty good. He got a diary. One day my father came out of the tent and he say, "This morning my son get back to Allakaket. They get back about five o'clock." Edward wrote that down.

When they come out Oldman and up to Allakaket Edward showed me his diary. He wrote, "This morning your daddy say you come back five o'clock in the morning to Allakaket." I tell him that's right. We travel all night, get back April 27 five o'clock. How did he know?

Yeah, he knows. That's their business, you see. That's what you call a medicine man.

Married to Lydia

I lost my first wife in '31 by TB. People were dying with TB that time. I came down here to Cutoff the next year to get married again. There was three girls I could get married to, but two of them their father was White man. My mother say, "You might as well get married to someone can speak our language."

I knew Lydia from before when I spent one winter trapping around here. We stay here and hunt muskrats all spring. Then we went down to Nulato. She was adopted down there once and they baptized her

Lydia and Edwin Simon Collection

Lydia Simon and Edwin Simon with a pike 1933.

Catholic. So we got married by a Father down there in Nulato.

That summer I built a house a few miles up the Huslia River for Lydia's parents and they gave us their trapping cabin about fourteen miles from here. We stayed there trapping thirty years. When that first house got rotten we built another one and just added on to it. We had two-room building down there just like this one here. After that we build another house again at fish camp. I built lots of houses in my life. Everywhere I'm going to stay I built a house.

Sam Dubin

Sam Dubin had stores string all along this Koyukuk River. He had a store down Koyukuk Station, Dulbi, Hog River, Hughes. He had a store in Allakaket, Bettles, and Wiseman. He was a Jew and he was a money-maker. Real money-maker but he's kind lots of ways. He never write. He can't write. Didn't know how.

First he traveled by dogs. Then around 1918 when he bought out N. C. Store in Allakaket, he got the *Teddy H.*, little steamboat. He had bunch of people working for him on that. He hauled his own freight

Selina Marie born in Huslia 1956.

and the mail.

But you see he couldn't write and it got to be too many smart people with him. He'd get money from the Indians all right, but the White people took advantage of him. I could see what's coming in 1924. People take advantage over Sam Dubin.

He was all right but, say, if marten is twenty-five dollars, he'd pay fifteen dollars for it. Because he's the only one got store up there. And if we say something, like if I say something against him, he'd say, "Edwin don't come in the store no more."

That the way he was. He was pretty good man, kind, help anybody. But that's the way he want. He's big shot and he don't want nobody talk against him.

One year, 1922, muskrat prices really drop. They started out at three dollars and went way down in the middle of the season. Sam Dubin was at the mouth of the Koyukuk River when he heard about it. Right away he sent somebody up with gas boat to Hog River. Jack Sackett was running the store there. They sent a Native guy, Louis John, all the way up to Allakaket by canoe. Ross Seghers had Sam Dubin's store there.

We came out early and we already sold our rats at three dollars. Last people to come out were too late. Prices was already down. But N. C. Company still had the store in Bettles and nobody told them the price dropped. So those people take their rats, three or four hundred each man, go up the Alatna River little ways and pack them over to Bettles. They sold the whole thing for three dollars to N. C. Even bank went broke that year. Lot of people went bankrupt, broke on that.

Sam Dubin was a money-maker but he went broke too before he died. All his store close down. Allakaket and Bettles store burnt

Lydia and Edwin Simon Collection

Martha Oldman and Abraham Oldman taken in front of Wilfred Evans' store in Allakaket 1933.

down. The *Teddy H.* landed on a stump in Nenana and he lost it. And these people working for him cheat him. Take advantage of him because he can't write. I knew then it was important to read and write.

Dominic Vernetti

Dominic Vernetti is another storekeeper. He had store and big warehouse in Koyukuk. I always think he was better man than Sam Dubin. He was married to this half-breed Indian woman, Ella Vernetti. He was Italian and he was a money-maker too. He's another one couldn't write. Yeah, he could write a little Italian but not English. We didn't have any airplane in here and he would help us out that way.

One time in the spring around April, Richard Derendoff got sick. Young man not married yet. He got real sick and he couldn't walk. Lot of rats then. Jack Sackett was at the store. I ask him, "You going to take care of Richard this spring?"

He said, "No, I'm taking care of nobody."

I talk to people. Sidney Huntington and lot of people. I said, "We can collect rats and send Richard to Tanana to the hospital."

"Okay," they said.

So I wrote to Dominic, "Send up plane. This spring when we come out we're going to collect rats and pay you up." One fellow took that letter down to Koyukuk Station by dogs on the crust. Three days later airplane come. Pick up Richard. Took him to hospital. That saved him.

Spring before we go down to the mouth, I got a bill. I collect all the rats and a little more and I give it to Dominic.

Another time Bobby Vent got sick so he couldn't walk. Got something wrong with his knee. Summertime. I went up to him, say "Bob, what you going to do?"

"No money," he said, "Can't do nothing."

We had mail plane land here, *Mudhen* we called it. I went up to that plane, said, "Hey, take this fellow down to Koyukuk." And I write to Dominic. I tell him I got to send Bobby down. Send him to the hospital in Tanana. He couldn't walk. He was sick, pretty sick. And I say in Thanksgiving I'll collect mink and pay you back. Send me the bill.

They took him down to Koyukuk and Dominic sent him up to Tanana. Dominic took my word. He was good that way.

Never Brag

I used to tell story, you know, talking. And down Galena, Sidney Huntington ask me, "Why don't you tell good side of your story sometime? How come you tell all bad luck story? When you had hard time?"

"Well, that's all I remember," I tell him. "Because we had such a hard time in there then I couldn't forget that hard time I had. That's all I remember." See, I make excuse. I never say I used to go head of John River. All over. I kill brown bears and things like that. I did every summer, but I never tell. I never talk about it. Not one time I ever kill something. That's our way. That's Indian way.

Lot of people come home from trapping, never say, "I catch twenty mink, twenty marten." They never talk nothing like that. "Oh, I got a few skin," they say. Just like me when I trap, I never tell people how much fur I catch. If somebody ask I say, "Oh, I got a few skins."

Stephen Attla is the same way. He makes four or five thousand dollars every year trapping. He never tell nobody what he got. He's superstitious. When fur buyer comes he takes him over to his house to sell his furs. He don't want nobody to talk about what he got.

    Some people say I kill this much. I kill lot of fur. Brag. We don't do that. Eskimo is same thing. I was in Kotzebue and asked them. They don't talk about it. But they got to be good man to kill them whales and things like that. Jimmy Huntington, Sidney Huntington, three or four of us went over there about twelve years ago. We got weathered in with four Eskimos. We cook beaver meat, give them supper, and we stay up all night talking. We asked them about their life, how they killed whale. They wouldn't talk about it. They're like that. Finally I said, "Well, we're the same way. Suppose I go out hunt someplace, I don't say I killed this. We're superstitious. I guess you people is the same way."

    This old man say, "Yeah, that's right. That's the way we are."

    We cannot brag. I prove it one time. We were all going down to our camp on Fish Lake. Trap beaver in February. I said, "We don't have to haul meat down. Lots of moose down there. I'll kill moose." You think I kill moose?

    I set beaver traps, snares, then when it's windy, I go after moose. Sometimes I just see it go that's all. One good sunny day I was walking in Fish Lake and hear moose cross in there. Fresh track. I have .30-30 carbine and I want moose meat bad so I walk in there. Moose short ways. Two-year-old cow. I tried to shoot. My .30-30 wouldn't shoot. I shift the bolt. Wouldn't shoot. Wouldn't work. Can't shoot. I fool around, make noise, pretty soon he look at me. Then that moose run in the brush. I look in there, fool around with the gun till it shot. I walk home, sit down, take my boots off.

KK'ułk'eeyaggazee

I used to be good runner. Run down caribou two or three times. I get to the right side of it so I can shoot with right hand. When the caribou jump like, I run along side and just drop every one of them. While I run I put shells in there. I done that lots of times. .30-30 is just right. .30-06 is too heavy. I leave all my brothers. They can't keep up with me. I run in snowshoes pretty good. Lee, my brother, was man, married already, but he was younger than me. He might have keep up with me, but he break his snowshoes. I run after that caribou six miles. Six miles. They get kind of run down and I started to shoot them. I got sixteen one time.

Caribou has got leader. His neck is rubbed both sides. They call him *kk'ułk'eeyaggazee.* He's the fellow that watch out. He drill his caribou. They come up to him and they rub his neck with their horn or head. And he's just skinny, poor. But when we chase caribou he's way ahead all the time. Way ahead. Even how much snow it is he's so tough. That's their boss. If you knock him down, they get kind of lost. They don't know what to do.

Me and Oscar Nictune hunt caribou together one time. "*Gganaa' gganaa',* partner," I say. "Shoot the leader." Oscar was good shot. He shot the leader. We ran after them. We shot quite a bit after we shot the leader.

Wind Is His Boss

Long time ago people used to just try to run everything down. They used to run down moose and run down caribou. They don't know how to hunt moose or caribou because there was no moose and caribou around here much. My father told me they go up to upper river people around head of Old Man and South Fork. When they got up there, here's people hunting moose! They don't go out after moose when it's cold weather. When it's good wind, south wind, warm, then they go out hunt moose.

My father say, "Moose. Wind is his boss. He go by the wind. That's all." Wind. Moose. Wintertime. And caribou is the same way. When caribou feed around in wintertime, wind is their boss. Well, my father, here is upriver people, Allakaket people, old people long ago, South Fork people. Here them people here, they hunt moose with the wind.

You see, if somebody walking in his track, he's going to smell him. Every time moose start to lay down if wind this way, he go this way. Come back and lay down here so if anything walk in his tracks, he'll smell it. So people when they hunt moose, they leave the track and hunt it with the wind so moose can't smell them. Sometimes four times we leave that track, come back to it. Then if the track is yesterday, we see him first time we look for him.

We have to be quiet. If moose hear the dogs or hear shot, they run about twenty miles. Leave that area. Right now, nothing. New style. They come right across from the village with all kinds of noise. That's the way the animal is right now. Animal get so used to noise like airplane and kickers.

First time I went hunting moose by myself, I made lots of mistakes. You made little mistake, then you don't get that animal. But once you make mistake, you remember. That's the only way you learn. I must have been twenty years old, young. Before I was married. I was hunting moose alone and I see wind this way, south wind. I stay on the side all the time so he can't smell me. Every once in a while I go back to his track. Here he run! My! How he smell me? How he see

Lydia and Edwin Simon Collection

Big William and his wife from South Fork of the Koyukuk River 1907.

me? I started to run after him. Terrible big wind, you know, and so he thought maybe if somebody follow him he'll fool that fellow. That's what he did with me. I made mistake right there.

He never see me. He just run from here to maybe far as Franklin's house. Then he lay down. He wanted to lay down from big wind so he run. That's what he do. Fool people. Then where I see he run, I want to run. I run after him making all kinds of noise. And here he just lay down. Then he hear me and left.

When I got home, I was staying with my folks yet, I told them the story. "Oh yeah, he fool you right there," old man say. That's what they do. Big wind come, they run and then lay down. If somebody is hunting them he going to smell." That's one mistake I remember good. When I see he run I supposed to walk in one more circle and don't make noise. If I walk maybe just one time then I would see him. Same when they eat. They walk fast, then stop to eat. You follow him, he'll smell you when he eat.

First Moose

First time I shot moose, oh, big animal. I hunt with people lots before I was out with myself. I must be about nineteen or eighteen years old. It look pretty big. First thing I do is dig down in snow on one side with snowshoe and tip him over. Tip him over easy in snow. Then cut the head off and cut him all around. Skin him. And cut in every joint. Clean the stomach, everything. Then shovel the snow off in there down to the ground. Put him in there and throw lot of snow in that meat. Cool it off. If you don't throw snow in there it going to get kind of spoiled. Then put the skin over and pile snow on top. Next day we haul it.

Sometimes we clean the stomach and save the blood in there. Tie it up and freeze it. That's for the dogs. But that's what they used long ago for tea. People use it. They cook blood. My mother cooked blood. Boiled blood to drink. She take a little crushed snow to test if it's done. Put crushed snow in there, look at it. Pretty soon, that's done. I don't know that part but that's what they used to do. They drink blood just like we drink coffee or tea right now.

I took so long to cut that moose I didn't come back till one o'clock in the morning! Come back walking after midnight. I finally got moose. I different from all my brothers. My brothers was all lucky people. They start to kill something when they are young. But me, I had kind of tough luck to start with. I was big boy, eighteen. I can't kill nothing. But I always try. Never give up. Never give up. The more I can't get nothing the harder I work. Just like I used to all my life. Even right now, if I started go after moose, want to kill moose if I can't get him, I just stay with it. Stay with it.

So I told them I shot moose. "No wonder you was gone a long time," my mother say. "How you butcher it?"

I made a mistake that time. When we skin moose, they want us to leave lots of meat on the skin. Half inch of meat so when they start to scrape it that thing come off easy. If there's no meat it's hard to clean it. People never threw away moose skin those days. They got to tan that skin or make rawhide out of it. They clean it with a moose bone scraper. Cut the leg bone and file the end. Then make birch handle and make a good one. If there's lots of meat it just comes out easy.

"Oh my!" she say. "Don't you know any better? What's the matter with you? You know we got to have lots of meat on this moose skin. How I'm going to clean that moose skin? No better than that!" she say.

After they scrape the meat off they turn it over and shave off all the hair. Then if it's cold weather they take it outside and stretch it on the snow. They make holes on the edge and use stakes to hold it stretched out. After it freezes they tip a sleigh over, put the moose skin on top, and scrape it. A bunch of womens do that and they get all done in one hour. When it's all clean and just white they hang it up in the wind. Then my mother used to tie it good and put it away in a gunny sack. They keep it clean. If the moose skin gets dirty then it's hard to tan. If it gets wet it's hard to tan.

In the spring they start to tan the skin. They got the moose brain they keep in a can for a long time. It gets kind of sour. They put the brains in a washtub or basket with some water and the moose skin. There's just a certain way to do everything and if you make a mistake on that then it's hard time. Some womens put moose skin in just one time, then they rinse it. Tie one end to a tree, put a stick in the other end, and twist it till all the water run out. Then before it dry they hang it up and scrape it with a rock to make it soft. Then they make a little willow fence, put a couple moose skin over it, and make smoke under it. Dry rotten wood. That helps it tan too.

No Moose Around Here

I was raised up around Allakaket where there's lots of moose. But when I come here never hear of moose for years. Long ago when they see moose track in wintertime, people run the moose down. Camp two night behind, chase that moose three days. Never hear of much moose around till around 1945.

One year, falltime, we were down at Fish Lake. Franklin was getting big as Gallee is now. I start to hunt bear on second of October. First snow a couple days ago and here's moose track! I couldn't believe myself! First time I see moose track around here. I know it's moose track. And just down here little way I was working all morning at gas boat. It had a kind of twist so I was blocking it up to level it out. I made lot of noise. But moose went this way. Three. Where they come from?

I been down here how many years never see moose track around this river no place. Well, I walk up looking at bear hole and I came back to the river up there to see which way they go. No moose track. I came back on this way—and nothing. They're still in that area. I had .30-30 and I got five or six shells. That's all.

I start hunt that moose. They're in there. They never run. All that noise I made working on gas boat. Pretty soon thick brush I was walking and here they start to run. Three of them. I shot three of them. I don't know for what. Just because first time I see moose for years. I had meat all winter.

After that lots of moose started to come. Moose get so thick they die off. Dead moose all over around here about four years ago. Wintertime. Liver trouble, I guess. Something wrong with them. Anything get so thick they die off. Beaver done the same thing.

Used to be lots of beaver around here thirty years ago, and they started to die off. One beaver house five or six beaver die right off. Then three or four years after beaver die off from what they eat, I guess, moose started die off too. I don't know why. Firefighters drop borax but that's not around here. Something that eat brush, willows. They're the ones die off. Like rabbits, there isn't much rabbits no more. And beaver. And moose. I don't know what the cause. We never heard in our stories that animal die off. Except rabbit when they get so thick they cycle.

Tracy Derendoff, Clifford Simon, Edwin Simon and Gallee Simon, Huslia 1978.

Through the Ice

It was the sixth of March and we was pretty near done with beaver. But Franklin got sick with flu and he got few more beaver house out yet. On the fifth, I took Lydia down on his sno-go pick up trap for him. He caught beaver. Next day it turn cold. Twenty below with north wind blowing. I tell Lydia too cold for her on the sleigh. Too far, sixteen miles. "Let me go alone," I tell her. "I'll be back one o'clock. Wouldn't take long. Just one snare."

I had muskrat skin coat with corduroy cover. I put that on. If I kept it on I wouldn't be here today. Lydia had a high-priced down coat I got from Outside for her Christmas present. She say, "Use my jacket. Warm. Too cold," she say. "This is warm one."

"Aw," I say, "I got my jacket on already."

"Oh," she say, "that's all right." And she take my zipper down, take my muskrat jacket off. I put on her eider down jacket. That saved me. I had wolf skin mittens with Ouside rabbit liners but I got little cold going down.

I drove up on the ice and turn around. Walk over to the beaver house. I should have tested the ice. Well, I thought it was all right. One snare over there, one snare here. Two snare, he said. Just right. I look, then hit that ice two times with the chisel. Poufffffffffff! Ten feet by twelve feet ice just cave in!

Blackfish. That blackfish suck all that ice front of beaver house. Here I was falling in the water. First thing I do is swim back to edge of beaver house but the snow is about foot and a half there. Drift. Try to get out. Couldn't do it. I try and try.

Pretty soon I see another snare. Little birch right across the water hole. It's the toggle, but I couldn't reach it. Funny, too, I got no knife. I used to have knife in the belt all the time. No knife. That's why I'm stuck.

I talk. Everything I think. I thought I never see people again. I got no way to get out. And if I get out I'm going to freeze anyway. So I said, "Well, I'm seventy-one. We got to die sometime. It's no use to try," I say. "I'm glad I go to church all my life." And I say, "I never hurt people. I don't have to worry." That's what I say. Everything I think, I talk. "It's all right. Person have to die."

I see that snare over there. Then I clean the snow off the ice. Break the ice with my elbow. It keep breaking. Pretty soon I reached over there and grabbed hold of that stick. I pulled the snare and the end got caught in the ice. Hang in there pretty good. I roll that stick and tie the snare on my wrist. So I'm not going to drown.

I'm going to freeze though. Half in and half out of the water. First when I fell in the water I took my false teeth and I threw it up on the crust. And my red cap. I threw it out there so they'll know where I am. I never thought I'll see people. But I keep trying. Keep trying. Try to pull myself out. I lean on the ice. Rest for a while. Then I clean off that ice about two feet long, half a foot wide. Clean all the snow off. This last I'm going to try again.

I kind of pull myself little out and started to kick with my feet. Just like swimming. I move my leg and got one knee on top of that ice. But I'm scared. I thought it was going to break. I'm going to fall in again. I don't know what I did. Suddenly here I was laying down on the snow. I don't know how I got there. I still got that snare tied to my arm. I took it off. Then I said, "Thank God." Well, one thing I wouldn't drown. Now I'm going to try to get home. To town. Four miles anyway. Four miles is least on main trail.

I say, "I wouldn't go far. It's all right." I try to get up. I couldn't walk. My leg was numb. I crawl over the snow. My mitts is wet, everything. I look inside the sno-go and here's old moose skin gloves. No lining. No canvas gloves. Just old moose skin gloves in there. I put that on. I talk. I pull couple times and it went. I start to drive.

I got to the trail. By the time I got to Big Lake, I see ice in my mitts. No choice. Keep on. I see water running from my sleeves. And boy, I'm all just chunk of ice. Glizzard. I put one arm in by the engine. I'm going to save this arm, I thought. I'm going to lose my hand. I had no choice. I drive.

About three miles from here I get on the hill. Down lower end of hill little this side. I pass out. I hit the throttle and run right off the trail. I wake up, say, "No. No." I started to talk. Then I squeezed that thing. Right there I started to hold both sides good and talk. Words come out. I was just going to black out. "Too close to village. Too close to village. I'm going to make it. I'm going to make it." Just like I sing. Never quit.

Bobby Vent, my neighbor, was cutting wood. He see me coming. Talking. He run in to Mary, that's Lydia's sister. "Something wrong with Edwin!"

I drive up to old house and my daughter come out. She holler. She look at me. Big chunk of ice. Bobby come down. People run in there. They break me off. I got to the porch and Lydia met me. "Honey I never thought I see you again." That's all. I pass out. They leave me alongside the stove.

Twenty below! I travel sixteen miles against north wind! They cut all my clothes off me. Pretty soon I come to myself. "*Snaa.*" They were holding me. They put their mouth on my nose and mouth so I could breath. Pretty soon I see. I look. People in the house. All full. "How long I been out?"

"One hour and ten minutes now you're out. Plane will be here pretty soon from Tanana," they say.

I was in Tanana Hospital for three days, that's all. This hand is no good. Freeze my knuckles, but not too bad. That's all that happened. When I came out of the water I got my hat and put it on, but my teeth isn't there. They went back and got them for me. Thirteen feet of water they measured. And sixteen miles I drove. People don't believe it. I was seventy-one. Funny I never lose my hand because nothing but big chunk of ice in there. Water run from in there and it's glizzard, but I got no choice. I have to hold that throttle.

Eddie Bauer jacket save my life. I wrote to them, sent a picture, and they send me another parka again for present. They had my name in the Eddie Bauer catalog for one year. Why she took that muskrat jacket off? I would've sunk right now. I just wasn't going to die. I had canvas boots with fur boots inside. Caribou skin socks and khaki pants. All that freeze but water inside stay warm next to my skin.

Edwin and Lydia in a couple parkas made by Lydia, Huslia 1972.

Fish

We used to set fishnet under the ice down Fish Lake. They call it *Łookk'a ts'ilyaanh dinh*, "fat whitefish lake," in our language. It's about fourteen miles from here. We have a cabin on the bank just little ways back from the lake. When the ice is about four or five inches thick we put fishnet in there and have fish all winter.

We make holes in the ice about five feet apart as long as the net. Then we tie a rope on a stick and push it through from one hole to the other until we have that rope stretched all the way under the ice. We tie the net on the rope and pull it right along until it is hanging under the ice. When we look at the net we pull it out and it drags the rope back in. To reset it we just pull the rope back out and it will pull the

Fish Lake Camp 1953, Franklin is putting iron runners on the sled. Franklin Simon, Dolly Simon, Selina Simon, Eleanor Simon.

net in. We hold each end in place by tying it to a long pole about twenty-five feet long and sticking the pole in the mud. We have to keep the net about two feet under the ice so the floaters wouldn't freeze to the ice. If that happens we have to cut up the net or lose it.

Rich fish we got. Awful rich. Lake fish is awful rich. But right now the lake is going dry in there. Cotton trees growing on the edge where there used to be water. Lakes is going dry around here.

Lush is the only one I hear people say wouldn't travel in bad weather. Stormy weather not much fish in fish trap. But when it gets clear they catch lots of fish in fish trap.

Eskimos make fish trap little different than us. We put fence across from both sides of the river and funnel in the middle. Then we put poles all around the funnel so the fish swim in and can't find their way out. Then we cut a hole in the ice and hook them out. Only thing is you can't make fence on the main river. Dam the main river. Like the main Koyukuk River. Anybody do that, that man die all the time.

Last one did that was Eskimo living twenty-five miles below Allakaket. He wintered in there with his whole family. He dammed the whole river to catch fish. That winter he died. Never dam the main river. They dam side stream like Alatna River or Old Man Creek.

There's always some lush and some years we get a heavy run, but salmon is different. Sometimes salmon don't come up this river. Some years we get just five or six bales to a family. We used to get forty bales, two thousand fish, for our dogs for the winter. Takes a couple weeks to get that in a good year. Check the net twice a day.

Salmon eggs, fish eggs, is rich stuff. *Kk'oon' tolidla* they call it. That's what they used for tea. Just like drinking tea. Got to drink something. Summertime they cure the eggs and put them in birchbark

Louis Cleaver, weaving a fishtrap from spruce, bound with willow, Koyukuk River 1934.

Lydia Simon and Annie Vent in fish camp twelve miles below Huslia with a king salmon 1958.

basket. Tie the cover down with roots. Then they take a chunk out and boil it up. That's their tea and coffee, *kk'oon' tolidla*.

When I was a kid I stand right by my mother when she cut fish. I take that air sack from the salmon and blow it up. Stuff it with salmon eggs. That was my job. I hang them on an old fishnet and let them dry for a month. Sometimes I get hundred-pound gunny sack full of that *kk'oontseek*. In the wintertime I eat that. That's my grub. Lot of vitamins in those fish eggs. Not only me, all the kids used to do that. But no more. Now the Japanese know how good those eggs are and they pay high price for it.

Bertha Moses checking a fish net in front of Allakaket with her kids.

Teach Her How to Shoot

I married to my wife Lydia when she was sixteen. She never went to school. Never see schoolhouse. Me too. I went only first grade, but when I went down to camp, I start to teach her lot of things. First thing I done when we stay down there alone I ask her if she ever shoot rifle. No. Well, we go down to the bank and sit down. I had .30-06 and .30-30 carbine. I teach her how to shoot three or four times a day. Now she's as good a hunter as I am. Good shot. And the wonder is she can't see very good. But she's good shot. She even killed a bear right across the Koyukuk River with .30-06. She did that when she was down fish camp and I was working at the Hog River.

Last year she shot a moose. Every year she shoot moose with .30-06. I teach her because when we stay alone what she going to do if I go out. She have to be able to handle rifle. I tell this to people, young people. I say when you get married, if you going to camp out someplace, teach your wife how to shoot. How to handle gun. Have two rifles. What they going to do if bear or anything comes to camp?

That's what I tell lot of young people all along the Yukon too. That's what I do. And I ask Lydia what gun she wants. She shoots good with .30-06 so I always take the .30-30 carbine.

And she have to learn how to run kicker. She have to learn how to run sno-go. Supposing we go out together anything happen? There's one time about ten years ago somebody drowned up Minto. Going down to Minto from Nenana. A man and his wife. He try to start the kicker and it spin and he fell overboard. Drowned. His wife don't know how to run kicker. She can't. It just get all fouled up. Her husband drowned and she float all the way down to Minto.

I had inboard motor long ago. I teach her how to run it. Everything I do I teach her because we stay alone. Supose anything happen to me, she have to take care of everything. I tell them boys, "When you get married you teach your wife everything that you do."

And we go hunting together. Last fall she shoot moose up Dulbi. And I bought her a new .20-gauge pump shotgun. She shoots ducks and geese with that. Gallee has a .410 and he shoot a bunch of ducks. Bunch of ducks and geese piled in the boat going up Dulbi. Then we got moose and that's all we need.

CHAPTER THREE — Lydia

My First Parents

Lydia and Edwin Simon have lived together forty-five years and have been integral parts of one another's life. Chapter Three is part of Lydia's story in her words.

I was born in 1916 up Cutoff. My really parents is Francis Olin and Christine Olin. I was going to be Christmas present. Surprise for their friend, Rose Kokrine and Peter Kokrine, down Yukon River at Old Kokrines. My father, Francis Olin, say to Christine, "If you have baby you going to give it to them. That's how much we love them."

Lydia scraping the scales off big whitefish.

Mamma say yes.

Rose and Peter Kokrine used to come up here to Cutoff because they like their friends. They used to winter up here with my parents. Two or three family go over to Kobuk with dogs. Seven dog limit because of food for them. Kobuk used to be first town when they go hunt way over the mountains. Stay over there a month. Come back from around here. Two or three family do that.

So, must be 1915, before Christmas, Christine told Rose Kokrine, "Old friend, I'm going to surprise you. I'll give you Christmas present." Well, time passed and she forget about it.

Springtime. Way up in Cutoff on the lake, there's little short portage and another lake. That's where my really parents spring because there was lots of rats. This Rose and Peter Kokrine spring on other lake, next lake. So they camp while they are trapping rats and pretty soon I was born. April 25.

My parents keep me three days because I'm small. Then Christine tell Rose and Peter when they come over from other lake, "That baby's the one I was going to give you as surprise. That was going to be your Christmas present, but I had it slow. Anyway, I'll give it to you." Well, they adopted me. Peter Kokrine, big tall guy, pack me down to

Society of Jesus, Oregon Province Archives

Old Kokrines circa 191·

that other lake and that spring they come out and went down to Yukon, Old Kokrines. Rose and Peter Kokrine is my parents then.

Then I was between two and three years old. Just like dreaming, I remember little. Peter Kokrine say, "Well, she's going to see her real parents. Her daddy and mamma." I was thinking, I don't know what they mean.

So we went down the Yukon by Ruby. Went by Galena and come to Koyukuk Station. It's fall. We went down to Koyukuk fishing. Olin and Christine were fishing down there too. Rose and Peter say, "That's your mom and dad."

Then when I was about four or five we went down to Koykuk Station again for a potlatch. I know because Irma was baby that time. My sister Mary's first baby, Irma, and my mamma's last baby was same age. And there's my brothers Jubilee and Baynee. Sisters Celia and Mary. Four out of sixteen. The rest die before that. Now the only sister I got is Mary Vent. We're only two out of sixteen. Eight boys and eight girls.

I remember good that time. I had all white clothes and them black shoes with just like little black marbles all the way up. And silk petticoat with lace on it. I think I see myself but they say I was blind. It's just like a dream, but I thought I see that time. And they say I talk like White English, don't know how to talk Indian. It's because Rose Kokrine went to school down Holy Cross and she used to talk English to me.

At six years old I was big. They say I try to look, but too bright for me so I close my eye. They say I run around just like I see. Run all over and I know people, they say. By the voices.

About six years old my father, Peter Kokrine, start to get sick. I know there is hospital down Nulato at that time. We had tent outdoors on the bank. I know we stay there. Me and mom sleep on

Rose, Calman, and Peter Kokrine circa 1910-15, Kokrines.

the floor. Daddy was coughing. Nighttime. After that I never see him. He die. Next year my mother Rose start to have TB. She died too in Old Kokrines. There were lots of people in there then. Now there is nothing but grass and willows.

After my mother Rose Kokrine die and I stay with Old Man Tom (Jean-Marie) and Grandma. They're old. We stay in camp in slough. They thought I might disappear so they always sit me right between them. When we go to the boat I walk between them. Between them all the time. They hold my hand too. They like me so much and it's just like they're going to raise baby. That's why.

So we were in the slough in little cabin. I remember we had spruce boughs on the floor and poles bed, poles table. Nice little clean place. We sit down behind the stove and they were cooking spruce chicken in oven. Boy, I was thinking, gee, I had nice mamma and daddy again.

They tell me to call them Grandma and Grandpa. But there's Ellen Henry that call them Mamma and Daddy. They raised that one. I hear her call them Mamma and Daddy and think that's their name. I call them same way.

I stay with them over one year. They baby me. Talk to me in Indian. Pretty soon salmon run. We're staying in that same little cabin in slough again. Hayman comes across river from fish camp. No kicker. Just use paddle and lumber boat. Poling boat they call them.

He say, Joe Stickman from Nulato was coming up with little steamboat. He tell Grandma and Grandpa, "Lydia's parents went on down Koyukuk River to Koyukuk Station." I start to think. So that's where my Mamma and Daddy is. I want to see them right away. I didn't understand I was adopted and that's not Rose Kokrine he talk about. I just want to see them.

Ellen Henry, Mr. and Mrs. Tom Marie Kokrines 1918.

I see Grandma and Grandpa was crying. They sit down on the bank. Cry. Hayman put my clothes in sack and put it in boat. He went across river with me to wait for ride on steamboat.

I stay with Hayman five days I guess. I start to cry for Grandma and Grandpa. I say I want to go across, see Grandma and Grandpa first. Brother Hayman say, "No, Joe Stickman is going to come around pretty quick. He might miss you. You sit down right here and take care of them two kids, hold them." One of those kids was Evelyn, Mrs. Sanders Cleaver. I call her sister since that time. Hayman went around the bend to pack wood while I sit there.

Pretty soon we heard that boat coming. It's Joe Stickman. Tall man. He tell me, "Your Mamma and Daddy want you down Koyukuk." I want to go down. I want to see them right away. And

Laura Pitka, Catherine Pitka, Edward Pitka, Hayman Henry, Elizabeth Henry, Lena Demoski, Robert Demoski at Huslia 1946.

I miss Grandma and Grandpa too. I got all mixed up. So he put me in the boat and lock me in one of the little rooms. I guess he thought I might go overboard because I was blind.

He land in Kokrines, land in Ruby and Galena. Every place the bank was just full with people, not like right now. Them womans want to see me. They say, "Oh, that's Lydia Kokrine." Used to be my name. "Oh, we want to see her." Joe Stickman pack me up the bank and around town. He don't want me to walk. I heard lots of people talking about me. Talking about my mother, Rose Kokrine, Peter Kokrine.

Joe Stickman put me back on boat and say, "We're going to go to your daddy and mommy, your real parents." We go on. Stop in Koyukuk. There was lots of people. Joe Stickman pack me up the bank and say, "Here is your daddy and mother." Boy, they talked different! Some words is different kind of Indian. They don't talk like us. I start to cry. I say, "I want my grandma." I don't want them.

They hold me. They love me. But, no. I cry for three days. I say I don't like them. I want to go home to grandma, I call them daddy and mamma. My father, Olin, say, "Aayyyy. I didn't know she's blind. I wouldn't take her back. I let her raise up there." He feel sorry for me, that's why.

So I sleep by him for one week. I hear him. Nighttime they make medicine for me so I'll see. He's medicine man. He give present to other medicine people so they help. You know, high-priced stuff. So every night they made medicine on me. They don't make medicine in daytime. Never. Just nighttime.

The ones making medicine is Little Paul. He was small man, crippled. That was Lavine Williams's daddy. And Old Man

Stickman, Joe Stickman's father. And my daddy, Francis Olin. Three of them.

Every morning they say my pillow was just wet. You know, water come from my eye. Pus or something. Every morning for one week. And afternoon I start to look. Open my eye, but too bright. I close them back. And after one week, all at once I opened my eye and I could see. Everything! But if I see something too long time it's two. And sometimes I could see it and sometimes I can't see it.

I'm like that right now. Sometimes I can see airplane from far away. Sometimes I can't see it, even if it's close. And people, I can tell by the way you walk and your voice. And I could tell from your clothes if you wear same thing. But if you change clothes, lots of times I wouldn't know you. I got cataract on my eye. Maybe that's why I

Old Man Stickman and Kriska with Nulato Jail in the background, 1910.

sew close. My sister and my aunty tell me, "You should quit sewing. That hurts your eye." But I can't. That's just the way I am. Since I was seven or eight. Since that time I open my eyes, it never change.

But I shoot good. I have to find the sight right away and shoot. Fast shot. If I wait too long then I can't see. I have .410, I shoot that one good. I don't miss so far. I hit it just like accident. Even .22.

On Fourth of July, two years ago, we try to shoot balloon across on the bar. They tie it right on top the water with stick. We had pistol. Try and shoot target, five shot. I shoot it fast, automatic. By accident I shoot one, I guess, holler! And last year, Fourth of July, we had big gun, .30-30. We all shoot five times. I got one on the third shot. Balloon out there on the bar. It's just by accident. And all my life, I shot five caribou. The horn I got up there on our cabin, that's one.

Daddy Had Two Stores

Pretty soon I get used to my really parents. And there's my brothers and sisters, Jubilee and Baynee. Celia my younger sister was taller than me. I was just tiny, skinny. And Mamma adopted Catherine Attla, her grandchild. We're five kids. Just like big family for me because I was raising alone before that.

I like them. I try to talk like them. They say, "*Eenaa, Eetaa.*" *Eenaa* is mamma and *Eeetaa* is daddy. So I say something, but when I talk with them they laugh at me because I talk different.

When they took me back we stay in fish camp till September. Two, three family is in them camps. Daddy had camp all over. He had camp down here, fifteen miles, Fish Lake. He had house in there close to ten years. He had camp up Dulbi River, way up on the flat. Summer we travel with boat. He had good scow. It was big scow with Kermath engine, you know, them chug, chug, chug one. He had four bed in there and table. We had stove in there too. We put bundle of fish in there and move that way.

That fall I go back with them, we move up to Cutoff. Dominic Vernetti tell Daddy, "I'm going to lend you stuff so you'll sell stuff for me. You'll have little store for me. Half and half." Daddy say yeah. So Dominic give him lots of stuff. Fill up scow.

So we move up there. Daddy start making new big house the spring before, 20′ x 24′ or 22′ x 24′. The ridge pole was on already. Daddy finish it that falltime. He's been gone down Yukon River all summer. Well, he finish house and fix it up for store. He make counters and things like that.

Daddy open store. First time we stay in town for winter. Daddy don't know how to write. But my sister's husband, Larson Charlie, know how to write a little. So he write in this thick book. It's credit book. You know, to give people credit. People trapping don't have money yet. He give them credit so they can outfit for winter. There's about eight families. Big families though. There is Big Charlie and Little Charlie. Little William, Mr. Happy, Hog River Johnny, Daddy. Around by March he was doing good. He bought lots of fur. So he give out outfit again for spring outfit.

Pretty soon Ambrose from Kokrine come up. Tall man. Lazy guy. Come up and stay with Daddy. March I think. I know it's long days. Well, they used to make home brew and they were drinking. Daddy scold Ambrose. Tell him he just stay with daddy and eat. Do nothing. Never even cut wood. Daddy start to chase him out. Ambrose took that big credit book and put it in the fire! Dumb!

No credit book is pretty hard. They have to guess how much credit people got. Larson kind of know. Well, Daddy don't like it. Too much trouble. They divide up money and spring he wants to go out camp. Better. We eat good out camp. Fishing and everything.

We stay out camp all summer. Move to camp for all winter. They go to town for Thanksgiving day. Gone for five days and come back. We got outfit for about three months. They got hundred pound flour, hundred pound sugar, and about fifteen pound of rice. Mamma know how to cook it. She save it.

Christmas we come to town. One month ahead we'd count the days. One month is just like one year to us kids. Right now one month is just like one week. Just like money. Them days we got quarter, dollar, we buy lots of things with it. Now it's just like nothing. Calico material was four yards for a dollar. Right now it's near two dollars a yard. That fifty pound flour was five dollars. Right now it's pretty near twenty dollars.

After Christmas we move up to the flat. Lots of mink, lots of rats, lots of beaver them days. We had no moose. No caribou. No big game around there them days. But lots of lakes. Big lakes with lots of rats. Them lakes right now are just dry. That's why we have no rats right now. After spring ratting we went down Koyukuk and summer down there.

Old Man Sommers, Sr., had big store down Nulato. His wife is Daddy's cousin so they're brother-in-law. Old Man Sommers say, "Brother-in-law, you want to have little store up there for me? Out camp. Don't have to be in town." Daddy say yeah. I was about ten years old.

Daddy haul stuff up Dulbi River, went down again and haul another stuff up. Go way up the flat. That big scow is old so Daddy tear up his boat. All lumber. And he dig a hole about two feet deep and build 18′ x 18′ house on top. They fix it good. No holes. They bank it. Make good roof with dirt and moss and birchbark so it's warm.

We got nice stove in house and lots of wood. Cold them days, fifty, sixty below.

He make big open cache for stuff. He had tent over it. That's where his store is. A few people from Cutoff would go with dogs and buy stuff. George Attla, Sr., and Sammy would come. He bring his fur and buy stuff. Tony Sam is his really name but we always called him Little Sammy. He bring about ten skins and get lot of stuff.

He got six moose skins from Mamma. Them moose skin was twenty dollars for half. He bought dress for Big Sophie. They talk Indian. He say what he want and Daddy say this much for fur. He's out there at cache looking at everything. There's mouth organ, shirt, wool jacket, even toys. Everything. Even you don't see toys around them days Daddy sell them.

When somebody come to store we always watch. My sister and brother were by the cache. I was standing by the door. Mamma was up there in the cache so she sell everything. Towels, everything.

Pretty soon Little Sammy take out a box. Cold. About thirty below in daytime. Sun is up. He say in Indian, "Gee, my kids would like this." It's mouth organ. Metal. He put it in his mouth and it stuck from cold! It stuck both side of his lips. Froze on his mouth. He say, "*Haa! Sodaa', gonaaa'.*" He say, "Ahh, Sister help me!" So my mamma tell him, "leave it in your mouth for a while so it get warm." Then, easy she tear it off his mouth.

Other ones come down with fur and bought things. Daddy pretty near run out of stuff after Christmas. That little fur cache he made was full of furs. But I know Daddy had his own mink. Eight mink. They had tent on the flat where they trap from. Mink track everywhere. Just like squirrel track or mouse track. Daddy told me.

My job that time was pack ice from across the river. Ice about eight

Lydia and Edwin Simon Collection

Tony Sam (Little Sammy) Big Sophie Sam, Bergman Sam in Cutoff 1932.

inches thick. I pack a big chunk. Fill up my packsack. We had washtub in the house for water, I fill that one everyday. Daddy say, "You see mink track across there?" I tell him yeah, lots of track under the ice where water go down. He tell me set trap for it. He tell me how.

Daddy gave me one trap, so I set it under the ice where lots of track is. I caught one mink. Daddy go across with me and he kill it for me. I was scared of it. After he kill it he tell me, "Now set that trap good."

Before that we catch camp-robin around the cache with snares we make for it. Daddy say, "That's for trap bait. Save it for me." He never say that's for marten.

So I set trap again. Same way as first one. I never catch nothing. Then I think, well, he say save that camp-robin for trap bait. I thought that was good for mink too. So I take camp-robin, leave it in that trap. Now I think I'll catch mink. I set it good. I never catch mink. Never catch mink. Finally Daddy sneak over to my trap and see it. He come home that evening. When they go to bed that evening, they talk. I hear Daddy laughing and tell Mamma, "My poor daughter. She just use that camp-robin for her trap. No wonder she don't get nothing!"

Next morning I ask Mamma, "Mom, how come Daddy say that?"

She say, "That's for marten bait. That's not for mink. That mink is scared at that."

So Daddy had two stores. Two winters. I don't know how he make out. Maybe he make a little money but we have big family. We eat lots. Well, I stop this far and tell you story.

Grandma Madeline's First Bread

My Uncle Hog River Johnny always tell us story. In springtime and summertime he always stay in tent. I call it his house. And when I got time and want story I walk up to his house. I tell him news before he tell me story. We had no radio them days. We had mail once a month. No mail plane. Sam White go up by boat and bring mail. That's the only way summertime. Wintertime is by dogteam. So I tell Uncle Hog River Johnny news what we hear about in letters.

He always call me *sitłaa'aa*, because I call him Uncle. *Sitłaa'aa* is like two brother's daughters, what you call niece. Well, he say, "*Sitłaa'aa,* I am going to tell you story because you always want story from me. And it's really true story."

I say, "Yeah, that's what I come up for."

He say, "I was kid. That was long ago. My mamma was young and she was widow. She never get married after she was a widow. They call her Big Mamma. She had a lot of kids too. Half-breed and Indians. She looks like quarter-breed. She looks pretty too. Madeline is her name. (Baptized by the name Magdelen, but people called her Madeline.—E.J.)

Well, this Hog River Johnny is Indian. His sister is Grandma Bessie here in Huslia. I think she's younger.

Uncle Hog River Johnny say, "This time there was three of us. Mamma, Bessie, and me. I was small. Mamma's working fishnet from them willows bark. For salmon. They know how to work at it. they know what kind willow. Nice, straight willows. Thirty-feet-long net. They caught salmon in there.

"We had birchbark boat. Nice big strong frame out of good birch trees. Cover that with birchbark. So we're out working net. We see one White man coming down from Bettles, or Wiseman. Someplace up there. He come down in little boat. He say he give us half sack of flour. Mamma don't know what this is but she listen. She learns fast.

"This man tell her to put baking powder and salt with this flour. Stir it with water and cook it. He give her little can of baking powder and small packets of salt. This White man talk with her. She understand everything too.

"She tell us kids, "*Nok'aghanuhłt'usk!*" ("You guys put something into shape."—E.J.) She mean, make it in them birchbark bowl. White man tell Mamma what to do and she tell us do it. How to make bread. When she said, "*Snaa,* ("My child—E.J.) *nok'aghanuhłt'usk,*" I stir it long time and move it with my hands. Mix it good and make it hard. Shape it.

"Mamma got fire under smokehouse by the door. That's where she cook. No stove. They don't like stove. First time people see Yukon stove, every one of them buy one. Then they leave it in the cache. They don't care for it. They make hole by the fire. Cook in there. Dig hole about three feet long. Mamma put bread in there. Cover it. Cook in there.

"They got no pans. No mixing bowl. They got few cans for teapot. From someplace. They never lose it. Use it for years and years. Few people got them old-style bucket. Them thick enamel, metal bucket. But it's high price. They have to buy it from each other. Sometime they're really good friends and they give one to their friend for present. That's prize. They use bucket for cooking and one can for campfire teapot."

Grandma Julia and Old Man Simon's New Tent

I hear other stories about new things that was coming in long ago. You know, like that Yukon stove everybody buy. Grandma Julia, Edwin's mamma and Old Man Simon had fur. So they buy a new tent. Cheap them days. Everybody buy one. Grandma Julia and Old Man Simon buy little stove too. They haul it far as their camp.

There's lots of snow. They smash snow down with snowshoes. Then they put spruce boughs and put up that tent. Put little stove inside. That's first stove. They always make fire on ground before. Well, they start to freeze in that tent! They say, it's no good. They don't like it. It's not good for the way they live.

They hang that Yukon stove right under a big tree. They don't want it. And that brand new 8' x 10' tent. They tear that right in the middle. They put poles up and wrap those two sides of tent around so there's hole on top. Then inside tent they dig snow down to the ground so they can make fireplace under that hole.

When they leave that camp, Grandpa, Old Man Simon say, "No we don't like to haul that tent. No dogs to haul it. Three dogs is the limit. Let's put it under the trees. Cache it. When we are moving back this way we're going to haul it to town. Sew it together in summertime." Some people don't like their tent, even summertime. They lived outdoors summertime. Tent is too hot. But Grandma and Grandpa Simon sew theirs together in summer.

All Circle, Hand, Hand, Circle

Daddy tell me story about how they used to dance. Cutoff. That's before they take me back from Kokrines. Christmas night, New Year night, they dance all night till six o'clock in the morning. Daddy, Mamma were young them days. Big Charlie, Little Charlie, Little William, Happy. Tom Cook was dark fellow. Canadian. He was married to Aunty named Julia, I guess. Tom Cook played violin. Mamma used to play accordian a little. She learn from Tom Cook somehow. Somebody else play guitar.

They dance and party all night. They make home brew. White Mule, what they call. And Daddy used to know how to sing all kind of song. Eskimo song, and they dance like Eskimo. When they go over Kobuk they learned that. They just teach each other.

All these people don't know how to speak English too good. And toward morning Big Charlie say, "Well, everybody die tonight, Eeeeee!" What he thought he say is, "Well, everybody dance tonight." They all want to learn how to talk White English. So this other guy try to beat what Big Charlie say. They don't like to get beat them days. They think they're smart and they want to be even. So this guy say, "Square dance! Square dance! All circle, hand, hand, circle. I call. I call."

So they all got partners. They hold their hand and start circling. This guy call for square dance and say, "Well! I call, I call." He say, "Fifty cigarette an join an hand an ladies an sicaven light an tovido." Everybody stop. They all stand and look at each other. They don't know what to do! They don't know what he say. Only Tom Cook just keep playing violin.

And that's the time they drink home brew and stay up all night at

Lydia and Edwin Simon Collection

Mr. Happy, unidentified, Francis Olin, unidentified, taken in Koyukuk 1918.

Christmas, New Year party. They play cards too. They play gamble. What they call Jackpot and Casino. When they play cards we stay home every night in one house. They play in Aunty's house and Mr. Happy's. They stay up till six, seven o'clock in the morning. We cook hotcake and wait for them. Finally they come home, eat, and go to bed. Sleep till eleven.

 That Aunty, Aunty Lucy, was Daddy's older sister. That one's husband make good Indian song. They help each other make song. Aunty drowned in muskrat house. They were trapping muskrat in March. Early one morning Aunty put on snowshoes and check trap she had in muskrat house. She kneel right by that muskrat hole and fell in the water. Drowned. They find her snowshoes was upside down, floating. That's because blackfish suck that ice and make open place and thin ice. I remember her little.

Bear in Hole

 Long ago, but not too long ago, I was kid that time. They say one woman was nice woman. They call her Leasa Bidok'idniyh. Her husband is Johnny Bidok'idniyh. Both of them, they never get mad. They're nice people. They just talk nice all the time. They never talk about nobody too.

 This man, Johnny Bidok'idniyh, he caught bear. Black bear. In the hole. In the falltime when they're in hole, they're really good meat. That's the time we really need it. In falltime they're hard to find. A few people, that's all is lucky with it. You know how it is if you lose your needle? If you can't find it, you wouldn't find it. If you could find it you could find it. That's how they hunt bear. Like some people is just bad luck with it. Can't find bear hole. Johnny

Bidok'idniyh was lucky with bear. He always find them falltime.

In falltime there's lots of bear holes. Bears fix them up so they could move in. They get grass and put it in hole. Sometimes he pick birchbark and go in hole with that too. That's how they get it ready when they move in, falltime, before it snow.

One time Edwin was in camp. Falltime. He was hunting seventeen days. Go out everyday. Start six o'clock. Come home to camp after twelve noon. Hunting bear. He look at bear holes and bear holes. No bear. Then he walk on mountain and find bear hole that's new. You know how he find out it's new? He see it's full of grass by the doorway. He can tell that bear pull lot of grass before he go to the hole. That's the way they find the bear hole in falltime before it snow. They say, "*Doogh zo k'itsaan' dik'agheeł'eek lonh, hadnee.*"

("There's sign of something (bear) picked some grass around here."—E.J.)

Arthur William (in tent), Julia William, Effie William, William William, Lydia Simon in Hughes 1951.

Well, Edwin say he look inside hole and see that grass was not inside. Bear never pull it in. He just leave it by the door and hole is open. And here Edwin see bear feet is sticking up. There's two of them! Two bears is just stretched out and dead. Just like a man Edwin say. Mother bear and one year baby bear.

People say that's *hʉłaanee,* superstitious, when it's like that. Daddy used to say it's like mamma bear is helping her one-year-old baby make his house. Mother bear bury him. Just like mother bear bury him for somebody. That's what they say. They say when somebody find that kind, one of their relatives is going to die. *Hʉłaanee.*

The next year after Edwin find bear in hole his mother die. She was around eighty years old. And last year Paul Derendoff find one. His brother drown this spring. "*Baanh yineeneełneegee,*" ("One that was buried by it's mother."—E.J.), that's what they say. They say mother bear bury him. Few people find them kinds. It's true. Lots of old things is true. Because that's our stories from way back. Lot's of things is *hʉtłaanee*.

Bird and Animal Songs

One thing I like to tell from our old stories is these bird songs. Bird songs and animal songs all come from our old stories. Those stories is too long so I just tell you little bit. Tell you those songs Indian way.

Like this robin, you know, the one with the red chest. You could hear the way it talk Indian talk. It say, "*Dodo silinh k'oolkkoy ts'eega' teelzuk teelzuk teelzuk. Dod silinh k'oolkkoy ts'eega' teelzuk teelzuk teelzuk.*" It means, "My brother-in-law told me to swallow them pike guts, pike guts." Sometimes it just say, "*teelzuk teelzuk teelzuk.*" ("Slurp it down, slurp it down, slurp it down."—E.J.)

There's other story about bird talk. Well, this young girl got handsome husband. Handsome human being. Well, this young girl has jealous grandmother who raise her. She's jealous of this handsome man. So everyday this man go out and hunt. Bring home chicken, rabbit, everything.

One day, when he's out hunting this grandma say, "Grandchild, I'm going to comb your hair. I'm going to fix your hair up." Grandma start to comb young girl's hair. While she's combing her hair she pick up skin needle. Pretty soon she stick needle in young girl's ear. Break the eardrum. Kill her. Grandma bury her under the tree someplace and dress up in all her grandchild's clothes. All because she want her husband.

When her husband come in in evening a bird land right by him and talk. This bird talk with him and say, "*Sitsoo, sitsoo, sidzey hʉłaghudla gheeyits. Sitsoo, sitsoo, sidzey hułaghudla gheeyits."* It's this man's wife. She turned to bird and tell him, "Grandma, grandma, she break needle in my ear. Grandma, grandma, she break needle in my ear."

Another one is small bird. You know that winter and summer bird. Tiny one. Chickadee. She say, *"Sik'idziyaa eehulaa ee toon' toon' toon'."*

Wolverine Songs

Well, all the animals used to be human being in them old stories. Wolverine was the big chief. He died so all the animals start to make potlatch for him. That's where potlatch start. All the animals make song for wolverine.

Really big owl make song for wolverine. He say, *"Taa'aa o bits'inh k'akuh ts'iłłaalinh łonh. Taa'aa o bits'inh k'akuh ts'iłłaalinh łonh."* ("Father from whom we chop fat has gone," meaning father who was a good hunter and brings home fat game that we chop, it's fat is gone.— E.J.) He means, grandpa always get food and it's fat all the time.

This really big owl, not night owl. Big owl, *nigoodzagha,* we call. That one never lie. We hear him talk in camp falltime. He always talk. He really talk true. He was kind of medicine man. He never talk for nothing. He's true. He make song for wolverine. But I don't remember his song. And this night owl, small owl make song and say, "*Yoonaanaa loo loo loo. Yoonaanaa loo loo loo.*" ("Way outside, loo loo loo. Way outside, loo loo loo."—E.J.) I forget what that means. It's hard sometimes to remember way far back when we was kids and they tell us story.

Like this cross fox song. It's long song, but I remember part. His song for wolverine is, *"Dee go dagheelitsaa'aa k'akk'oyeets'a honok'ak'uhghadilidiyhɨɬ dinh heeyo huyo heeyo huyo. Dee go dagheelitsaa'aa k'akk'oyeets'a honok'ak'uhghadilidivhɨɬ dinh heeyo huvo heeyo huvo.*" ("The place where mouse goes in and out of something's (animal) pelvic area carrying fat 'heeyo huyo heeyo huyo'," meaning that the wolverine was such a good hunter that he created an opportunity for the mouse to go in and out of the fat game that he catches.—E.J.) He means mouse is coming out with fat all the time, back and forth. I forgot the rest of that song.

There's lots of songs those animals make. When they make song for wolverine they talk about the best thing they think about. Best thing about wolverine.

There's some of us try to remember the old stories we hear. Sometimes we come together and ask each other parts we forgot. We know it but just like it won't come out. We have to help each other. Like Mary Vent, Catherine Attla, Angeline Derendoff, and me. We always come together. And me and Edwin, we help each other remember too.

Lydia using a *trabaas* to clean fish.

CHAPTER FOUR — Work

River Boat

Well, the last of the sternwheelers we had around here is the *Idler*. George Black. That Black Navigation. He had a sternwheeler. I used to be pilot on that. I started working the boat as deckhand. Then I take the wheel. I read the river pretty good. I was born in the river. So I should know. Any Indian. All the pilots is Indian. Because they know what is the river. They know when creek comes out there is few rocks and stuff through the river. You have to keep away from that. And they know when there's two cut bank on both sides of the river, bar is in the middle. All them things pilot have to know.

I worked three summers as pilot. Quite a while ago. Somewhere around 1937 and 1940. Koyukuk River. Black Navigation run mail for Yutana Barge Lines. I used to know every bend in this river. We look at the bank. We know where to cross. We know where the bar

Steamer Oil City that Edwi worked on for a while.

is. We know which way is the deepest water. Like this river, from here to Allakaket. You got to have something that draw less than 2½ foot for freighting. Jerry Riley from Nenana asked me and I told him.

Last time I work on river is about five years ago. Captain lost his pilot up Allakaket. This fellow, captain, come down with airplane and took me up to Allakaket. I brought the boat back down for him.

Six Years in Dredge

I tell you before I never buy gold pan. I used to work mining camp, sluicing. But I never find gold for other man. I just work for wages. I work at this Hog River. What they call F.E. (Fairbanks Exploration) Company, United States Smelting and Refining Company. They patent that ground during the war. They drill it and patent it.

I start work for them in 1955. I work in dredge for six summer. I was only one that stay right through. I earn $1.90 an hour, eight hours a day. I was making my social security and getting unemployment when I get home in the winter.

When I was working Hog River we had a hydraulic in there. They make some kind of dam to hold the water back on the flat about three miles up. Water come down from there in a pipeline for the wash. The boys used nozzles. Wash about ninety-foot bank. Wash that and find old beaver dam out of little spruce tree, ninety foot down. That little trees is just like rocks. Must be million years old. We find some seashells too. Must be what the Flood done. We know the Flood from our old stories. I seen that around 1960.

One time we was working at Hog River. About the third summer. We heard in the radio, "Young fellow shot himself down Koyukuk, commit suicide." But they never named the fellow. Well, everybody want to find out who. Some of the boys working come from Koyukuk. That might be their relative. So everybody is anxious to know. Who is this young man.

Next morning it just come to me. I tell them, "Maybe this fellow that shot himself is Yatlin." I don't know what makes me say that. His brother was working in there too. Georgie Frank, Joseph Yatlin. Well, Billy Sam and all them people tell me, "You think so?" I say, "Yeah. I'm pretty sure that's the one who shot himself." Next word we get, that's him, James Yatlin.

About fourth summer I work in Hog River I get sick. I don't know. It's just from the ground, I guess. I had a bad flu. I work nighttime. I come home morning and have to go to bed. In trailer house at Hog River. Fred Bifelt was there too. I got sweat and fever. I thought maybe tomorrow I go to hospital. Now I couldn't do it. Got to sleep.

I go to sleep and dream. Fred say while I sleep crow come. Crow sit on post in front of house all day, just say, "Kuk, kuk, kuk, kuk." Crow just stay there. Don't leave. My father used to know crow. Some medicine man know crow. That's his helper. When I dream it's about my father. Maybe he's helping me.

That night, I woke up. I wasn't sweat, nothing. Gee, I woke up good! I eat and went back to work at twelve o'clock midnight till eight in the morning. Next morning when I come home Fred Bifelt say, "Yeah, I know you was pretty sick. Just as soon as you go to bed that crow land. Stay on that post all day."

Well, I don't know why F.E. Company stop working at Hog River. I know they fill up that Hog River. All the way down, muddy. Kill lot of fish and things like that. So I think people stop them.

Huslia Community Store

I worked at store for couple summers so I understand a little about business. I run store for Old Man Huntington in Allakaket two years. And I run the store in Cutoff for Jack Sackett couple summers. That's how I learn. That's how I get to be manager in early sixties, top board member for this Community Store we got here in Huslia. First we call this Co-op Store but they said no, we might get sue because of Fairbanks. Right now it's Hustler's Co-op.

You hear about Ella Vernetti? She's married to this Dominic Vernetti in Koyukuk. Storekeeper. Ella's half-breed. We used to talk. "Well, Edwin," she'd say, "soon as Indian get few thousand dollars they start to walk in the air. They think that few thousand dollars is lot of money. No Indian is going to get rich in the stores. Unless they take care of what few thousand they make."

Jimmy Huntington was that way. He had store in Huslia before but go bankrupt. He was young. Make few thousand dollars and go out Fairbanks. Stay out there. Spend a lot of money. Walk in the air. Sure. He went broke. Young. He got to learn. Everybody got to learn.

Well, thirteen of us own this community store. We used to call it corporation store but it's not corporation. It's our store. Thirteen or twelve people put in money to start that little store about eighteen years ago. We collect five thousand dollars. Some people put in two hundred, three, four hundred dollars. I put in five hundred dollars.

About five or six years ago people start to think the store was going broke. It went down pretty bad. Bad managing. Boys steal and everything. Well, Sidney Huntington, Robert Attla, George Attla, Jr., and George Frank all sold out. We bought their stock. So there's eight of us own that store now.

We make lot of changes since the store pretty near went broke. Five years ago we got no credit limit. People owed store sixteen thousand dollars that time. So big fire, people went firefighting, make some money and start to pay up. Pay up thirteen thousand dollars after big fire. But we're short three thousand dollars. Well, we have meeting and say we'll give fifty dollars credit to each person. That's all. We hold credit down. That credit is what killed the business. We're foolish to give five hundred dollars credit to person.

We try to run store the way it's supposed to run. Every fourth or fifth of the month we have store meeting. We call it stockholder meeting. All stockholders get together and fix up the book. See what's got to be taken care of at store. I say, "We got to run the business right in order to hang on. We don't want to run the business Indian way. Potlatch. Make potlatch out of store, give things away. We got to make so many percentage."

It's hard. We're not business people. But we still hang on. Not enough education. White people go to school and learn one thing. Learn to be preacher or bookkeeper or work in business. What chance we got? That's what I tell our lawyer, Barry Jackson. I talk to him. I say, "We can't run business alongside White people."

He say, "Well, you people got your own store in Huslia for how many years? I suppose if you got into business with village corporation money, you people will hang on to it."

I guess that's right. We hang on to that store and don't take help from nobody. Two years after we start store, three man come over from BIA. They want us to buy stock through them and they keep books for us. Take care of everything. We told them, "We never even ask you people. We don't ask nobody to help us. You people just keep away from us. We're going to have the store the way we want it." They thought we were village council. We tell them it's not village council store. It's just thirteen of us stockholders put our money together.

Few years later this ANICA outfit come in here. First thing they do is take Effie Vent and put her through their business school. Rest of us don't know what's going on. Then next year two men come here from Outside. Seattle. It's that ANICA Company. They say, "We took over thirty-two Native stores in Alaska. They explain, you people buy stock through us and we keep the books for you. Manage your store."

"WHAT?" I say. I was surprised. Me and Cue Bifelt say no. We all say, "No, no, no. BIA tried to do the same thing. We don't sell out. You people just keep out of our store. It's no use to talk."

Well, one year after that, another man came over again. He want to try take the store. "That's it," I says. "You just leave us alone. We don't want nobody fool around with our store. We're going to keep that store or we'll go broke. We don't ask nobody to come in here! That's the way we started."

They leave us alone after that. That was five years ago. ANICA from Seattle. I don't know who runs that. But I know BIA used to help village stores in place like Minto, Nulato, Kaltag. Even with BIA they all went pretty low. Lot of Native stores went broke. But eighteen, nineteen years we got that store. Building up. Hanging on.

Firefighting

You know BLM get firefighting crews from all these villages. They get crew from Alaska but overhead people they bring in from Outside. Well, last summer I talk to them BLM people. I told them, "Why don't you people get Alaska people to be overhead people. Why don't you teach them Indian boys? Why should you get rangers and crew boss from Outside?"

I hear they have a school this year. One week in Fairbanks. They teach them Alaska people to be overhead. I know they take three people from here, teach them how to be crew boss. That's good. These people around here know how to take care of themself in the woods. They know about Alaska. It not like somebody new come from Outside and don't know how to get along.

Well, last summer BLM want me to be a camp boss up here for big fire. Oh, I'd like to go. My boy Franklin was mad, he don't want me

Lydia and Edwin Simon Collection

Huslia firefighting crew on the Manley Hot Springs fire 1969. Front: Edwin Simon, Sammy Tony, Mathew Henry. Middle: James Itta, Silas Henry, Harold Vent, Ed Henry, Patty Yaska, Earl Attla. Back: Sidney Henry, Percy Wholecheese, unidentified, Edgar Bifelt, Winker Bifelt, Al Yatlin, unidentified, unidentified.

to go. He told them, "Don't take Daddy out. He don't need no money to go out firefighting. He might get heart attack." When I ask BLM if they get me job they said, "Oh, Franklin told us not to take you out." So, in 1971 was the last time I fight fire. Over two thousand people fight fire in there. Twenty days we fought fire in there. I was camp boss that time.

Alaskaland Tourists

I work one summer up at Alaskaland. Nineteen sixty-seven. They called this hundred year's anniversary. Eighteen sixty-seven to 1967. I just tell story in that little igloo house they got down there. Eight hours a day I talk. Tourists just line up in that little igloo. Poldine Carlo was working in there too. Half Indians, some White people.

I start work first of June. I was supposed to work all summer. But this funny thing happen. Around July 10 or 15, I dream my wife Lydia call me. She say, "Honey, you better come home. Something's going to happen in there. So you better come right home." Eight o'clock in the morning, I'm in my room in Fairview Manor. Alaskaland got room for me there. I stay there by myself. Go to work twelve o'clock noontime till eight in evening.

Well, I think about it all that day. I never tell nobody. But I worry. You see, that spring I was cutting wood and knocked my wife on the head with tree. While I was cutting tree I thought she was behind me. But she walk over to where that tree I'm cutting is going to knock down. It fell on her. Cut her head. I thought she was dead. She was knocked out and I haul her home. She went to Anchorage hospital. They fix her. She stay there couple of months. If that tree was just little bit more on her head it would have killed her.

From Anchorage she stay with me in Fairview Manor. She stayed three weeks and then went home to Huslia. That's where she was when I dream about her.

Well, next day at work it bother me. I didn't dream it for nothing. I done that before. Always come true. So why my wife call me? I talk to Poldine Carlo in Indian. I tell her, "Poldine, I dream that your buddy Lydia called me and say something's going to happen in there, you better come home."

"Oh, that's just a dream. Don't believe it," she said.

"Well, I don't know." It bother me. I supposed to work all summer. Contract. Finally I start to figure out how I'm going to quit. About five days later I tell Poldine, "I'm going to quit." She tell me go over to boss, see him.

I tell boss I'm going to quit, he ask me why. I said, "This town is too much for me. Too much changing for me. Bother me quite a bit." I never tell him about my dream. I say, "I live in the woods all my life. That's where I belong. I'm losing weight you know." I was losing weight too because too much noise. I never had rest.

"Well," he say, "okay." So I get my pay and I pack up all my stuff parcel post. Call up somebody in town and they haul everything for me to the post office. Next day I took off for Huslia. Came home. One week after that, Fairbanks flooded. July, first part of August. People run around with gas boat. Kicker boat in street. Nineteen sixty-seven. They took everybody to University. All the roads to University flooded. The Tanana Trailer Court. Fairview Manor. All over.

Good thing I got home. That's what my wife call me. I asked her. She say, "You know, I dream about you. That's about the time I dream about talking with you. Second week of July."

Bilingual and Survival School

I teach bilingual school for couple years in Huslia. I teach them Athabaskan. I was in Fairbanks for month and a half to go to school in University. They tell us how to teach. Seven or eight of us. Then I go back to Huslia and teach kids how to talk Athabaskan language.

I tell them kids old stories on how to survive and what we learn when we were kids. I tell them in Indian. It's not easy to teach. Some kids don't want to learn and they make funny face at you. You know how kids are. I never, not one time I ever say a cross word to kids in two years. They learn and they listen to me.

If they do something while I was teaching I ask them why. I pull them aside and talk easy. Ask them why they have to break something. They say, "Just to be tough." That's the answer I get. Why they want to be tough? But you can't talk rough to kids. You

Jeff Vent, Virgil Sam, and Jeff Sam reading one of the books in the Biography Series in their high school class in Huslia 1981.

just have to talk to them.

Well, after I teach two years I get new boss come around and tell me different way to teach. She tell me what I learned in University was all wrong. Well, that was enough. I don't like how I have to learn different way to teach. I quit. Catherine Attla and them people say, "Uncle, you better teach our kids." But I say no.

Survival school is what I want to teach. Teach them kids how to survive in the woods. It's kind of hard on young people right now. When they finish the eighth grade they leave us and go to high school. At least four years they're out from us. Go to school everyday. They don't learn how to survive in the woods. They need that if they're going to stay here in the village to live. You could teach kids lot of things for their own good. That survival school is great thing.

Sophie Peters, Christine Wholecheese, Fredricka Kayutuk, Helena Bifelt, Pearl Henry, Sarah Vent, Huslia 1981.

Soon as we were about ten years old we start to go with our folks, hunt, trap. Four or five man go hunt and haul us kids in canoe. And in evening when people talk they tell story. They tell how to live. How the animal act. That way we learn. Listen to people talking. They wouldn't let us say a word. We have to listen. That's for us. That's for our future. That's our eductation, how to live in the woods. How to take care of myself.

I teach my boy Franklin like that. When he was six years old take him to trapline. Let him play around. Set trap. When he was twelve years old I make a little sleigh for him. I give him two dogs. His mother give him teapot. We say, "You go down that way. You're going to trap. You make fire. Even if you're not hungry. You make fire and put spruce bough down the way I do. Don't let your moccasin get wet." He caught twelve mink and seven beaver that winter.

All these boys here that never went to school learn this way. Tony

Edith Bifelt, Ronnie Yatlin, Eddie Vent, unidentified, unidentified, John Sackett holding the fish, Eleanor Simon, Rosie Simon, Michael Simon, Emily Simon, Percy Wholecheese, Huslia 1958.

Sam, Cue Bifelt, Franklin. Franklin only went to fourth or sixth grade. They know how to live in woods. They go out with their folks.

This generation now is changing. Just like water in eddy. They just go around like that. It's too much changing too fast. They have to go away from village and when they come back home from high school they're kind of lost. Lots of young people kill themselves over it too. They don't know how to get along in village. They don't know how to survive in the woods. Summer, between school, they think that's their vacation. They don't have to work. They think they're smarter than me because they go to school.

Maybe after while the next generation will know what to do. I think they'll make it. There's lot of young people that want to learn our culture. They don't know how to start. But they'll help each other out. Nobody's going to make White people out of us. We're Athabaskans. Nothing can change nationality.

Well, this winter I'm on the school board (CSC). They elect me again. This winter I told Regional School Board, "If you want to spend money and take kids Outside someplace, why don't we take kids out to trap? Show them how to make fire. How to survive in this country?" No. They rather send kids around to race, play basketball, things like that. At least in summer they should take kids out. School District do little of that. It's just like summer survival school at fish camp. Teach them how to take care of themselves in river. More of that would be good.

You have to know lots of things in order to live in a village like this. If you don't know how to hunt. If you don't know how to trap. If you don't know how to make a sleigh or snowshoes or sew or tan skins, fish, what? You can't buy everything. Everybody have to work. Do it yourself in order to survive. If you're going to live in

Edwin comparing nylon fishnet with the old style ones.

Fairbanks, okay. Lots try it out there, but very few stay. Our young people come back here. It's for their future they learn how to survive.

Old Age Pension

It's kind of hard for us old people. I retired. About ten years ago I started to get old age pension, social security. For couple years we lived pretty good on that. Lydia, me, and Gallee. Everything was cheap. Now I'm getting same thing, $415 a month. Now it's kind of hard. We had oil stove little while, but we pulled that out. Cost too much. We can't buy fuel. And with running water, $35 a month, and gas for sno-go or kicker at $90 a drum, it's hard. We got to pay for coffee, flour, all that kind of food. It's the old people that get beat up. We're just struggling.

But my parents never got old age pension. Nothing. We used to take care of our old people. We kill meat for them. Give them flour, sugar, things like that. Anybody that's in trouble. People help. Like if anybody got sick and no money. We collect money and help them out. Even now. And we never buy a piece of meat from each other. I never buy a piece of meat. I never sell a piece of meat to my own people. That's the way we help each other.

Edwin and Gallee (Calvin) looking over the cache, Huslia 1978.

CHAPTER FIVE - *Nik'inla'an*

Somebody Shoot

Rosie Simon, Gallee Simon and Edwin Simon hunting moose 1968.

I never see woodsman, but every spring he used to shoot. We lived down Fish Lake about fourteen miles from here. Every spring I hear somebody shoot. Falltime too. One year I was making snowshoes and Lydia was sewing. Franklin was about ten years old. He was playing outside with his sister Amelia. No ice in the slough yet. Last part of September. I had canoe back to slough. Fishnet in the lake. Pretty soon I was working, shoot!

"Oh," Lydia tell me, "Franklin get hold of gun outdoors."

I went out. Here he stand look back there. "Who shoot?" I ask him.

"Back here," he say.

I stand in there. He look back. Stand in there. What in the world? Who's that? We stand there. Then we come back in the house and leave the door open. I start to bend that birch. Shoot again! I ask Franklin, "Shoot again?"

"Yeah," he say, "back there."

I grab .30-30 carbine. I shoot couple times and I holler. Somebody must be coming. Nobody. I walked back to my canoe in the slough. I paddle up this way and that way, all evening. Making noise and shoot. Nothing. Well, I say, that's what we call woodsman.

They come mostly in the spring. They hole up in the fall. They den up someplace. I don't know where.

Before that, first time I hear shooting, it was .22. I walk back to my house. Get my .30-30. It's about ten o'clock. World War II was on and I thought somebody got lost someplace maybe. GI maybe go in the woods. I told Lydia, "Well, too bad. If I see anybody and they can't answer, I'm going to shoot him. Because he have no business to be around here."

I walk back about half mile from the house. I stay under the tree till twelve o'clock. I had flashlight, .30-30 and the trail. Nothing. I never heard nothing. I came home, have coffee and stay up for a while. Who's that shooting?

One time Billy Sam and me were down below camp, hunting muskrat. Somebody shoot across the river. Two times with .22. Always .22. We shoot. Somebody coming up. Well, who? Must be people long way down someplace. He shot again. We took canoe two or three miles downriver. We never saw nothing. That's shoot again for nothing there.

Last time I hear woodsman shoot was about ten, twelve years ago, maybe fifteen. We went down to camp. Me, my wife, and kids. I went out hunt muskrat. I was strong yet that time. I dragged lumber canoe back. About five, five thirty, I come to that long lake where I'm going to hunt that night. There's beaver house in there. I put my paddle down. I'm going to sit and smoke for a while. Put one foot on the beaver house. Shoot! Little way. .22. Kind of deep lake with high bank. Hill. Ptooooo . . . ping! It go in the water like that. I stand there. Ptooooo . . . ping! It go in the water. Little way from me.

Heavy timber in there but I know there's nobody around there. I say to myself, that's him. That's him again. I sit down on beaver house. I smoke. Then I paddle under the bank. I never shoot muskrat. I didn't make noise. Maybe he know I'm there. I don't know. I paddle up to narrow little place. Narrow lake goes into that deep lake. I land and crawl up. Look in on the deep lake. I thought

I was going to see him this time. You think I see him? Nothing. That's the woodsman for you.

Stephen Attla, he's the one that pretty near see him. Just like a whirlwind. He says when he was young, him and his daddy hunt beaver in the spring. They come up on a niggerhead flat. They come up to beaver house. Shewwwwwwwwwish! They see brush just moving back of the timber. They went behind brush hump and look. Stephen is just about to sit down and he see shavings. Little shaving in there. Woodsman cut birch. That's the closest they ever see him. *Nik'inla'an.* Indians call him *Nik'inla'an,* woodsman.

One year we was down here hunting muskrats in the spring. Lots of rats. I killed thirty, thirty-five one night. Five o'clock in the morning I stop on a low bank. When it got hot I had little light blanket, that's all. I lay down between two banks about chest high so the sun won't hit me. Hot.

I woke up about three o'clock in the afternoon. I was going to smoke but I lay back down. I smoked pipe them days. I'm barefooted. Shot gun right there. Old twelve guage pump. Loaded in case of bear or anything. I had rats and duck and crane for dinner with me.

Pretty soon I hear somebody walking. Two footed. Two legged man. That hill. Well, here he come. I know that's not bear. Now. I always figure I'm going to kill him. I don't know why. What makes me want to do that? He don't want to kill me? But that used to be my idea. I grabbed the shotgun. Jumped right up there on that bank. Ready to shoot. Nothing. Nothing. Not even see winds like what Stephen say. Whirlwind. Nothing.

I had adopted girl, Adaline. One time she and her husband stay with us. We stay at camp at Long Lake, below Fish Lake. We go out to look at muskrat traps. Four dogs. And my son-in-law has four dogs himself on the other side of the slough. Pretty soon I see muskrat swimming on the open water. I tell Franklin to hold the brake. I go ahead of the dogs and I shot the muskrat. I told Franklin to come. He started to come and Ptwewwwww! Bullet from the brush just miss his head. It went right in the water. He started to cry. Gee, he get scared.

I run back in the brush. I say, "Who's that? What's that?" I talk Indian, I talk English. I talk everyway. Nothing.

We come home and rest. That evening I told him, I say, "I'm going up there. Take .30-30. See what it is." There's always shooting in there. For years. I tell Ben, my son-in-law, "Don't go up. We'll let the rats go tonight. I want to see that fellow. See what's in there. What's around there anyway." So I went up. Take a lunch.

I had new butcher knife, hunting knife. I just bought it that spring. I take .30-30, not .22. Up there is narrow place you can look way up and you can look way down. I got on this side under the tree. And I stay there four hours looking for him. Never see nothing.

About two o'clock in the morning, I got kind of hungry. I started to make fire. I put lots of dry willows in there and I sit down. I start to get my matches. Nothing. My matches is gone! My new butcher knife is gone too. Everything in my pocket is gone. Everything disappear. That's him. I don't know how he could do it.

There's one woodsman around mouth of Old Man Creek too. Another place people hear shooting and things like that. Just in the one certain area. I don't think they fool around close to the village. Maybe he got about ten miles square land. We don't know where he den up. Where he go wintertime. They say he den up someplace. Hibernate.

One family stayed at *Totohudaatłninhdinh*, good place to fish. It's about ten miles up Old Man Creek. Nineteen eighteen. They turn their pups loose. About eight months old. One disappear. Never came home. Couple years after that me and Johnny Oldman are going to camp around there. Springtime. We hear dogs. Somebody licking dog over there. Dog holler. "Look at that. White man got lost," we say. We walk over. Nothing.

Later, Johnny and me go out hunting rats. My wife and his wife got fishnet across the slough. Where lake comes out to river. They had to to across the slough with boat. Every night dog pull that fishnet out and take fish out.

When we come back, they say look at that. Their dogs are tied up. Never untied. And we see dog track in the mud by the net. Dog. We used to have gramophone to play records. Me and Margerite. I play that and watch for a couple nights. I watch for him. I watch for that dog. He never come back. Soon as we get back, no more. He keep away from that fishnet. Except when only womens are there. I watch couple night. Look through the window. Look through the door. I don't know what makes me think I'm going to kill him. I would shoot that dog, I guess, if he ever started to fool around with fishnet.

I'm not scared of him because he don't want to kill me. Lot of people is scared of him. But I'm so used to that. He's just shooting. I don't know where he get shells. Down at our house we never lock. I used to put shells and stuff in the house. Then I write down what I got in the house.

In the fall we move back down there. Everything is there. I look at my paper. Nobody steal nothing. I do that because this woodsman might steal shells from me. So I put shells, .30-30 shells, any kind of shells in the house up on the high shelf. Write down everything I got in there. I try every way. Try to find out about this woodsman.

Edwin Simon and family, Michael Lydia, Eleanor, Salena, Gladys, Dolly 1954.

Stay With Woodsman

There's an old story about woodsman. Long ago. I don't know how true it is but we got story about it. Fellow stayed with woodsman all one summer, one winter.

This young man went out hunting in the summer at the head of the river in the mountain where there's caribou and things. He was walking by himself. Pretty soon he see where somebody break limbs, tree limbs. He stand there. Suddenly he turn around, igloo right there.

He go inside. Here's man sitting down, fire to his back. Pretty soon he say, "Hello buddy. Hello friend. It never happened to you yourself? I'm so lonesome. I know you're close by me so I wished for you to come in. That's why you come in my house." That was woodsman.

So this young fellow start to stay with him. The woodsman doesn't go out to hunt. He just wish some more meat come in. Everything he wish and everything comes in. That guy stay with him all that summer and all winter. His people take him for dead. He never come back. He was young man. His mother and father, gee, they suffered. All winter. Nothing.

Next summer he started thinking about home. Then pretty soon this woodsman ask him, "Hey, buddy, you been thinking about home?"

"Yeah," he say, "I got parents, my mother and father."

"Well, if you want to go, you could go home. But don't tell anybody that you stayed with me. Don't talk about me. You never going to do nothing, but I don't know about other people. If people eat my grub, maybe I couldn't do what I'm doing right now. Maybe I'll go hungry then. We'll find out in a year," he told his buddy.

The young man made dry caribou meat. He make it up in a bundle and started to pack. Go back to his canoe. Pack everything down river. Went home.

He got home and they say, "Where you been?"

"Oh, I been out in the hills all winter. Live on meat," he say. He never tell them about woodsman. All that summer and all winter.

Next summer he went down river, down Yukon someplace. People tell him, "Woodsman come to village and he steal stuff. Fish and things like that so somebody kill him." He figure that's his buddy so he start down river to the village. Paddle all the way down and talk to his friends.

They tell him, "*Gganaa'*, buddy, this spring way early, woodsman come in here. He steal and somebody kill him. They build a cache for him. They dry him up there so people could see him."

When everybody sleep, this young man said to his friend, "Let's go up and see the woodsman. See what kind he is. I want to see him too."

He went up there. Yeah that's him. That's his buddy. That's the one he stay with all winter. You see people eat his grub then he can't wish and things don't come to him no more. That's what he figured would happen. That's what he told the young man before he left him.

Then the young man start to dance. He's got to kill them people. Lot of people get together in the spring and he got to kill them. He dance all night. He's a good dancer. Sing. People watch him. What a good dancer. Dance all day and all night. People just go to sleep all over. Then he started to kill people. He killed a whole bunch in there except his friend. He save his friend, that's all. Then after he kill everybody he went up the cache, get his buddy. He make a big fire and he burnt up his buddy. Cremated. That's woodsman story.

CHAPTER SIX — All My Life I Speak Out

Many of the Chiefs who also met in Tanana. Fairbanks 1915. Walter Phillips Collection, University of Alaska Archives, Fairbanks.

Tanana Chiefs

You see that picture of Tanana Chief long ago, 1915? I was there. I was seventeen years old at that meeting. All the chief from far as Nenana, far as Steven's Village, far as Nulato all got together in Tanana. Judge Wickersham from Fairbanks was Delegate to the U.S. Congress and he had a meeting with some of the Tanana Chiefs earlier in the summer. He told them there was going to be a railroad soon from either Seward or Valdez. He said there was going to be a lot of people come up when the railroad was done. No more game in the country. That's what Wickersham and those big shots in Fairbanks told them. So people have to have homestead, get the ground, or put Indians on reservations like Outside Indians.

That's why all the chiefs get together in Tanana. They don't want a reservation. All the chiefs talk. Give speech. Paul Williams and Theresa Butler were doing the writing. They're educated people through the Episcopal Church. High school people. They write.

No room in the dance hall or the mission. Only outdoors. About five or six hundred people there. They talk and then they write out to Woodrow Wilson. President Wilson that time. They wrote out that they don't want no reservation. All the chiefs sign their name. And that's when they took that picture.

That fall they get a letter back and have another meeting in Tanana. No reservation for Indians! And we could get homesteads on our places. That was good news. If we had reservation we couldn't do what we wanted to do. We would be corralled in. Just so much land for us.

I talk about land quite a bit after that when I go to meetings. I say hundred years ago my father live here. That's where I trap. I have cabin down there. And like that.

Tanana Chiefs started up again in the early sixties. We had a meeting in Tanana with Governor Gruening and all the big shots from Juneau. Alfred Ketzler was our president. He was slim young man then.

Then they moved it to Fairbanks. I put in a kick about it. I talked to our lawyer, Barry Jackson. We start this Tanana Chiefs down in Tanana. That's where the conference is supposed to be. Two rivers come together. That's where the old chiefs used to gather together. Just like you stole it from us. Tanana is the closest place for us to have our meeting just like long ago. History. He didn't say nothing.

That evening he talk to me. Barry Jackson, he say, "Edwin, that's good thing you say. Just straight out your shoulders and stand up and talk." That's what our lawyer, Barry Jackson, told me.

When the land claims were finally settled I really didn't care for it so much. It's all right for young people like Johnny Sackett and President of Doyon Limited and Tanana Chief. They got the money. But what we got?

Talk for Ourselves

Potlatches are the same now as when I was young. The people are superstitious. We have to do the same thing. Just like long time ago. Like when you tie a knot. You got to tie it the same way everytime. Very little change in Native potlatch right now. Sure downriver people in Nulato and Kaltag have stickdance. They have a different way and we have a different way up here. We're supposed to do that. But if you put a little change in there it'll be nothing left pretty soon. So you have to do it just the way it start long ago. Just like you tie knot same way. That's what our people do. See.

Fairbanks Native Association have a potlatch every year. One year I was Regional King and I had a Queen with me. They ask me to make a speech. I say:

> "When somebody make potlatch we always say thank you to each other. When somebody give us something we say 'thank you' and this person say 'you're welcome.' If somebody give us something we got to say something. We got to say thank you before we turn back. We don't just turn back and just walk away. Same thing at this potlatch. When somebody put lots of work to it. Lot of money to it.
>
> "Potlatch like this long time ago they talk to each other. They thank each other. They just don't come and stay back after they eat or nothing. They thank each other."

All my life I speak out.

Once they threw me in jail for having two traps out one day early. But that's my fault because I talk. They thought they would do something to me because I talk back to them but it just made me stronger.

I don't say, "Okay. Okay. You're right. You're right." I don't say that. If they say something I don't like, I talk back to them. I always think I'm here where my father used to be, where Athabaskan people used to be thousands of years. Nobody can't take that thing out of my mind that I think Alaska is mine. Hard thing to take it out of me. So when game warden or somebody say something to me

Lydia and Edwin Simon at home.

sometime, I talk back to them.

My father knew that when I was young man. *"Snaaa,"* he say, "don't talk to White man like that. White people is great people. We never talk back to White people."

"Well," I say, "why? I'm Indian and I'm proud of it. *Tłeeyagga hut'aan aslaanh.* ("I am Indian."—E.J.) Every nationality is supposed to talk for themselves. Otherwise somebody will just run over us." Just shake his head like that, that's all.

As I grow up I help White people. If they're right, I say you're right, thank you. But if they're not right, if they look at their side too much, I say you got to look at our side too. I told our preacher that one time. I help White people. If they say something good I say thank you for saying that. There's lots of good things that come from them and there is lots of bad things come from them too. Sure. That's right.

Equal Rights

I was working at Hog River, mining, dredge work, when they started to vote for statehood. We all vote. People vote for state or against it. I vote against. Sidney Huntington tell me I made a mistake there. Well, I thought there's hundred fifty thousand people in Alaska and Alaska can't take care of itself. We have got to get federal money to take care of us. That was my idea. But believe me I was mistaken. After it got to be state we're better off than before. We're more free and we had more to say for ourself.

When it was Territory everybody just run over us. No school. Everybody was just looking for gold, gold, gold. That's all. Money. Quick money and go back Outside. Nobody think of Indian around here. Like the State right now think more we exist. Them days, people never think we exist. That's the way it was. I used to talk to people. That's why they want to throw me in jail. If I keep quiet, just bend over and put my tail between my legs like an old dog, they wouldn't bother me. Sure.

Now when we come to State we're equal. We got same price as White people if we work. Same price. Long ago about 1920 when we work White man get fifty cents an hour, we get twenty-five cents. If White man get dollar an hour, we get fifty cents. If White man get five dollars a day, we get two and a half. And we usually do the work. I done that myself. I work for two and a half a day for I don't know how many years. Now, right now after the State we get equal rights. Now if anyone work alongside White man he get the same price.

Now Tanana Chief and AFN, our people talk for us too. See White man teach Indian, so Indian talk against them too. That's right. Equal rights. I believe on equal right no matter if Black or Brown or White. I believe on that. I couldn't get away from that since I grew up. Since I became twenty. I always believe on equal right.

I learned those things just being around people. I hear people talk. I got good memory and everytime somebody says something I think about it. That's the reason I quit smoking twenty years ago.

Bishop Gordon was here down at the mission house. We were sitting around talking. Our preacher, Don Hart, was there. He used to smoke too. We all smoke. Then the Bishop say, "You people don't realize how much money go up in smoke." He laugh.

I put that in my head. All winter I think about it. You people don't realize how much go up smoke, money. I started to figure out how much I smoke. In forty-five years I smoke five thousand dollars. Never quit smoking. Everytime when I trap, out sixty, seventy miles, one more night, no tobacco I have to go back to the village. I thought

I couldn't go without it. I have to go back how many miles.

So that spring in April I told Lydia I'm going to quit smoking. I got a hold of book about it. It says if you smoke long time that nicotine is in your system. If you stop you'll feel it too much. First week I smoke three times a day. Second week two times a day. And third week once a day. Three weeks time. I done that. When we started to go out to fish camp first of July, I leave all my tobacco, cigar, everything. Went up to camp without it. Get nervous. Chew on stick. Can't go to sleep. One week I lose two pounds. And on all summer. It took me two months to get over it. But I quit.

That's why I say when somebody says something I always think about it. I put it in my head. That's what I do all my life. If I work with White people and they say something, then I think about it, what they meant. If I don't understand then I ask them, "What you mean by saying that?" See.

Fifty Dollar Fine

Before it was State it was kind of hard for us. There was lots of graft. People travel round, they get money from Outside. Lots of game laws and they patrol us all the time. Game wardens had twelve or thirteen airplanes. They patrol us when we try to make a living.

We were living down camp. I had to take care of six or seven kids. We had a hard time. I went out on the fifteenth of November to break trail on my trapline. Season doesn't open until the sixteenth, but I saw two traps I hung up in a tree the year before. I set those traps.

Couple hours after I set those traps the game warden land right there. Ray Wulford. He took them two traps and he walk over my trail. When I come in here December 8th, he land here. He come to my old house and ask me, "Is that your trap?"

"Yeah," I say. I claim it. I don't want to lie cause there's lots of people trapping. I don't want to lie.

One year later, another game warden, King, came over. He said they're going to fine me $50. He said he'd take me to Ruby to pay the fine and bring me back same night. I say, "Okay," and go to the store to borrow $50. I don't have any money. Well, then instead of taking me to Ruby, he took me to Fairbanks and threw me in jail! He lied to me two times.

Fellow by the name of Dixie Hill was Clerk of the Court. I know him before. He's good man. He didn't like that. I told him they got to take me back to Huslia. He called up King.

I went to court the next morning. They ask me if I plead guilty on that trap. I say I already claimed it last year. Two traps day before season open. I paid my $50 fine and they took me back here.

Then Pat Kelly, our preacher, wrote two letters for me. One to Bob Bartlett in Washington, D.C. and to Governor Gruening in Juneau. Believe me, those game wardens caught hell for what they did. And I get even with King in Hughes.

There was six of them tagging beaver in Hughes during the dog race April 4. Lot of people there from Allakaket and all over. And people drinking whiskey, but I never took a drink for two days. I dress up good, take one drink and went into dance hall. I say "Stop the music for a while. I'm going to say a few words to these people here." Then I ask King, fellow that lie to me, "I'm going to ask you, King, why did you lie to me? You told me you was going to take me to Ruby and pay my fine. And two times you told me you were going to bring me back that evening. Instead you took me to Fairbanks and threw me in jail. I should have lied to you. I shouldn't claim that trap. But I like to be honest." I got sweating. All that time no noise. Nobody say

Lydia and Edwin Simon Collection

Little Sammy and Edwin Simon showing a white porcupine, an important omen.

nothing. Quiet. Just like you drop a pencil, you hear it.

Only one word he say, "Edwin, how long you going to remember this?"

"I'll never forget it," I tell him. You see, I stick my neck out because I was one to talk. I think I'm equal with anybody. Try to talk for myself ever since I got to be a man. That's why they do that. They don't do that with other people. They want to show me that they could throw me in jail. But it just make me stronger.

Two years after that we chartered a plane to go down to Koyukuk for a big potlatch. Big crowd dancing in the dance hall. Pretty soon here is King and Big John standing there.

"Hello, Edwin," he say.

"Oh, hello, King," I tell him. He reached out his hand. "Maybe I shouldn't shake hand with you, but I'm going to hold your hand for a while anyway," I tell him. I was feeling good. I drink a little.

"Well," he say, "Edwin I'm going to say something. If I know what kind of man you was I wouldn't take you to Fairbanks that time. I apologize."

"Oh, forget it," I said. "That's couple years ago." Another thing about when I bawl out the game warden in Hughes that time. I say something I shouldn't say. I don't know why I said it. I told them there's something in the air that's taking care of us. We're a poor people and you people punish us to make our living. That one who planned us here is taking care of us and will take care of you, game warden. I shouldn't have said that.

That summer the son of Clarence Rhodes, head game warden in Juneau, disappear. He and Stan Fredrickson, another game warden that was in Hughes when I bawl out King, were counting sheep with a big two-motor plane. They just disappear. Look all over. Can't find them. Gone

Pretty soon I see one big well-dressed man came on airplane. Jack Sackett had store over there. Me and Lydia were sitting down staying at home. That evening somebody knock. That fellow came on the plane. Overcoat. Well-dressed fellow. Necktie, everything. He come in the house. He ask me, "You Edwin Simon?"

"Yeah," just two of us there. I say, "Yeah, where you come from?"

"Anchorage. I came over to talk with you. Are you a shaman? A medicine man?" he ask me.

"Medicine man? Is that what you mean?" I say. "I'm not a medicine man."

"Well, I hear what you said to them game warden last April," he say.

"Yeah, but I don't have to be medicine man to talk like that." I said. "There's something in the air taking care of us. Whoever planned us in here is taking care of us. And when you people do that to us old people, he's going to take care of you people too for us." That's what I said. I mean it too. That's true. But I'm not medicine man. I walk right up to him. That's all he said. I never got his name.

Advise Doctors

I used to go to Public Health Service meeting four times a year. We help take care of the hospital in Tanana. We find out how the doctor treat the patients and like that. Help them do a better job. I talked a lot about the Village Health Aide Job. I said they got to get good pay for that. They spend their time in there. They can't go fishing. They can't go snare rabbit and things like that. They have to get good pay to hold that job. And you know, the second year I work on that it happen. Now Rose Ambrose gets good pay here. She goes to school for it and she does a good job.

Sometimes we had the meeting in Tanana and sometimes in Fairbanks. Once they talked a lot about drinking. All the first day and the second meeting. Doctors always kick about it. "Oh, you drink too much." or "you smoke too much." Things like that. Doctor always say, "You drinking?" I know because I been to hospital lot of times. They say I was drunk. Once I break my shoulder when I fell off my Honda. I wasn't drunk. But they ask me all the time. I say, "Yeah, I take a drink." Nothing wrong with that.

So I tell those people in the meeting. I say, "Over hundred years ago my people never drink in Alaska. Where did they learn how to drink? You people answer that question." They all look at each other. Never answer. I say, "You people brought this liquor to Alaska. You show my people how to drink. Now we got problem. You have to take care of our people too. If this man person or woman is alcoholic, you have to take care of them. Because you people teach us how to drink. Now if you think I'm wrong, I want any question about this." They all look at each other. Nobody answer it.

Speak for Whole Group

One young man wanted me to come to council meeting here one time. So I went in there. I told them, "Grandkids, *sakòykkaa*, grandkids," I say, "it's easy to go out and knock a tree down and work at that wood with saw. It's easy. But when you're president or mayor, that's hard work. Person have to be smart if he want to talk for whole group and think for whole group. Got to be smart people. You people don't know what you got into. You're taking lots of responsibility."

Nobody wants to take responsibility now. You can't satisfy everybody. I never was on council. I never was chief. After I talk to them they want me to be chief. I say no I'm going to retire. I want to take it easy. I don't want to take no responsibility for somebody. It's hard and they don't get pay. Bookkeeper gets pay. Accountant gets pay. But not chief. I think this chief business is going to die out in the villages. It's too bad.

About three years ago (1975) policemen and White people had a meeting here. They want to put policemen in the villages. Hire a Native for hundred dollars a month. I told them it's going to be just like stool pigeon. That's all. I'm not on the council but I have to say a lot of things when there's meeting going on. I think these are my people and I don't have to be chief to talk.

I say if you want to put in a policeman, you should build him a house. Give him a uniform and pay him same as you. Nobody is going to work for hundred dollars a month. It'll be trouble, that's all.

I lived in Tanana in 1915. They had a Native policeman there but it was hard. Make a lot of trouble. Little pay, about thirty dollars a month. Little jail house. You see we're all relatives. Every one of us is relative. Makes it kind of hard.

"I always speak out."

Cutoff to Huslia

When my first wife and I came down to old Cutoff first time to trap one winter, there was just five or six cabins in there. Not many people. There was Angeline Derendoff's family (Happy Isaac and Celia Happy), Lydia and her mother and father Olin, Tom Cook, Edith Bifelt's family, Big John and them people. Jack Sackett had a little store there.

We all came down from Allakaket, Sammy and George Attla family, Chief Henry family, me. People came up from Yukon River too. Richard Derendoff, Vent boys. Lot of Vent boys. So we were all mix up in there.

My wife Margerite and I rented John Evan's old store for the first winter. Later on I built a house in there. It was good village. Lot of fish in that slough. Everything. But it was low ground. Flooded every spring.

We couldn't get a school in Cutoff because it flooded all the time. After trapping I used to go into Fairbanks to sell my fur and I go to the newspaper. They had *Jessen's Weekly* then. It's *All Alaska Weekly* now. I used to put in the papers that we should have school. That was somewhere around 1940.

Finally they say if we move down to higher ground, move away from Cutoff, they could give us school. That's when some people move to Huslia, new site. 1949-50. No help from the government. Everybody move by ourself. We were one of the last ones to move here. We were staying at old camp, fourteen miles below.

Then 1952, we raft our house from old town (Cutoff). It was new house. We didn't want to leave it down there. We mark the logs, took it apart and rebuilt it in Huslia. Three people did that with their houses. We moved that same house a second time in Huslia when the bank cut. Those logs are still out there in front of this house.

That spring Episcopal Bishop, Bishop Gordon and school superintendent Dr. Ryan came over to have meeting with us. They say, "If you people build a house, we'll give you a teacher." So we built the house, log house. 1952 school started. And we borrow thousand dollars from the church for materials. We rent that building to the Territory for four years and got money to pay the church back. Now the Yukon-Koyukuk Regional School District is going to build

Lydia and Edwin Simon Collection

Marie Olin, Bessie Henry with two big whitefish, Christie Vent, Selina Simon, Amelia Simon, Chief Henry with a sixteen pound whitefish that Edwin Simon caught in Five Dollar Bill Slough. The Slough was named after a White man who lived there called Five Dollar Bill.

new school for us.

Compared to Cutoff, this Huslia is better country. Lot of fish and lot of game. High ground. Used to be lot of muskrats and lots of beaver. More sloughs and more fish around. You can go out and put a fishnet anyplace and catch all kinds of fish. That's why it's good country to live.

And not much people. After we move up here to Huslia more people started moving up from Yukon River. Now we got over two hundred enrolled in the corporation from here. We're 220 miles from Koyukuk Station, mouth of the river. No village between. And upriver, 180 miles to Hughes. So we have a big area. Good trapping.

We built this house we live in now about ten years ago. First thing we do in the spring we go up and cut the logs. We got 75 logs. Chainsaw it goes fast. We raft them down from way up Koyukuk River. They haul them up the bank for me with pick up. Then I start to work.

I work five, six hours a day all summer. Built this house. I was 71. Thanksgiving Day we move in and have open house. We cook something, have a little potlatch and dance. Dance till two or three o'clock in the morning sometime. Sometimes they have punch if they can afford it.

When I had open house I had a case of whiskey, case of wine, three cases of beer. I had money them days. Everything was cheap. I went down Galena and I bought case of whiskey, case of wine, and three case of beer. Everybody was here. Have dance and have a good time. My open house. That's the way we do. Yeah. People don't drink all the time in here, just once in a while. When it's holidays, or dog race of something. That's all. It's ninety miles to Galena and that's the closest liquor store from here. So once in a while people

Edwin and Lydia Simon and family.

Edwin Simon, Lydia Simon, Calvin Simon, Trudy Beatus 1973, in front of their new house.

drink. Not all the time.

In our way when we want to build a house we just go and build a house. After we moved down here to Huslia from Cutoff, BIA people used to come around. They wanted people to stake their ground. Put a piece of iron in the ground, survey it. Places they done that they make people pay. They came in here one time to have meeting about it. They want to put little piece of iron in the ground. Say we own the ground and make us pay so much. This was way before Land Claims. I got up at the meeting. "Who I'm going to pay?" I told these people. "I can move anyplace. Alaska is not settled. I don't want nobody to stake ground with me. I got a house already here. This is our old place in here, from way back history. My father and mother lived around here. Who am I going to pay?" That's a crazy idea. I asked them see if I'm right. I told them, "If you have anything more to say, say it." No they just look at me. Then they fold up and walk out. That's the end of it. In 1967, after Tanana Chiefs started, they paid back all those people that paid for their land in other villages.

This place used to be called Graveyard Hill because there used to be graveyard right here. When we moved the village we had meeting and we say we can't use that Graveyard Hill, we got to change the name. I told them this Huslia River comes out up here not far, why don't we call it Huslia. They agree so that's what we call this village here.

This is a good clean village. Easy to clean and no flood. This hill was all cranberries too. But a couple years ago they tear up the ground for running water. That's what makes so much sand right now. They dig all over the village. Put a pipe about ten, twelve feet down for sewer.

This place has an Indian name too, *Ts'aatiyhdinaadakk'onh dinh*, "place where the forest fire burn the hill out to the river." People used to gather here in the spring long ago. Gather here and play all kinds

Mary Vent, Norvin DeWilde, Lee DeWilde, Lydia Simon.

of games. I heard quite a few stories about this place. People from all over. Indians a hundred years ago. They come from fifty miles up and Hog River. That area. People used to get together here after breakup, after hunting rats. Come here, sing, play all kinds of games.

Lot of change around here. Like I say, I lived three different lives. First life is the way my folks used to live. We had no kind of power. We use birchbark canoe and poling boat. Let the dogs tow the boat or we pole up. Take our time but we make it. We never buy gasoline. We had coal oil lamp and candle. That's all.

Around 1930, we start to have inboard motor. Gas boat. Ten or twelve horsepower. And gas lamp. In 1950, we start to have kickers.

Then third life is what I'm living now. Around 1960, we get propane tanks, propane stoves, electricity and refrigerator. We even got running water to about half the village. Three different lives altogether. Now I don't know. I don't think I'll live fourth life. I don't know what's going to happen in 1980. We might get television.

Edwin and Lydia Simon waiting for a plane in Hughes.

Old Man Stickman c. 1910.

Post Note:

Edwin Simon died in March 1979. In 1980, television came to Huslia. In March 1981, Lydia Simon and Edwin's son, Franklin Simon, approved the manuscript for this book.

When asked if anything else should be included, Franklin said: "I wonder why he didn't say much about going over to Kobuk from old town (Cutoff). He used to go over there lots. He's got lots of friends at Kobuk and Shungnak, Charlie Lee, Chalie Sheldon, Henry Sheldon.

"I think what they used to do at this time in March was go hunt caribou and just keep going for maybe a week. Go to Kobuk, Shungnak, Kiana, Selawik, and visit Archie Forbes in Kotzebue. He even got his sleigh over there from somebody in Kotzebue. They called him Adabeena over there. (The name Adibin was used by older Koyukon Athabaskans who couldn't pronounce Edwin.—E.J.) They couldn't say Edwin, I guess, so that was his name.

"I was over Kobuk last winter. First time I went over there was '66 with snowmachine. Been over four or five times since. It's not that far, eighty miles. Now that would take me four and a half hours with sno-go. Two days with dogs from old town. And it's pretty good going because after thirty or forty miles there's no more trees.

"You know, he could speak their language too."

Edwin Simon was truly a remarkable man. Both as a unique individual and as an example of an era. The stories he could tell were only a small part of his experience. Behind the humility of many of our elders lie fascinating talents.

Edwin Simon made his ratting canoe but had to buy the aluminum boat.

Appendix A — Kinship terms

(From Eliza Jones, Alaska Native Language Center, University of Alaska, 1981)

Koyukon kinship terms (like body part terms) must be possessed, that is, they must have possessive prefixes.

When calling, addressing, or referring to someone, we use a kinship term rather than a personal name. When addressing someone directly, we use a special form of the kinship term called the *vocative*. Of the following kinship terms taken from the story, all but the first are vocative forms.

Koyukon Word	Part of Speech	Translation
baanh	noun	his, her, its mother
eenaa	vocative	mom, mama
eetaa	vocative	daddy, papa
gganaa'	vocative	friend, partner, associate
sikoykkaa	vocative	my grandchildren; used also to address a younger generation
silinh	vocative	my brother-in-law
sitłaa'aa	vocative	my niece, man's brother's daughter
sitsoo	vocative	my grandmother
snaa', snaaa', sidnaa'	vocative	my child
sodaa, sodaa'	vocative	my older sister
sozaa'	vocative	my nephew
tseek'aał	vocative	grandfather, word used in stories to call one's grandfather, still used in Lower Koyukon: this word is also a *noun* meaning 'old man' as used in Chapter One, "Bear, The Big Chief Stole the Sun."

Appendix B — Koyukon Words and Translations.

In order of appearance within the text. (From Eliza Jones, Alaska Native Language Center, University of Alaska, 1981.)

Koyukon Word	Part of Speech	Translation
Chapter One		
Dolbaakkaakk'at	place name	mouth of the Dolbi River and site of an old village
k'inaalnondinh, k'inaalnonh di	nominalization	(time) when people died
saanh	noun	summer
nin' yah k'itł'ina'	noun	mastadon, lit. "underground bones of something"
yoonaan hʉt'aan	noun	outside person, people
sinh taał, sinh taala'	noun	on which medicine people make medicine
oolneek	verb	he took
kk'ʉdaa	adverb	now
ts'aanok'ahootoł'olaa	verb	no one will become medicine person, any more
hʉtłaanee	exclamation	taboo!
Tsaalaatno'	place name	Chalatna on the map; possibly "Beaver Creek"
Aallaakkaakk'at	place name	Allakaket; lit. "mouth of Alatna river"
yʉhts'in', yʉts'a	postposition	towards you guys, you (plural)

kk'a nok'ahoonoditoł	verb	it (fate) will look back, meaning if a person does wrong to someone, the same or worse will happen to the offender

Chapter Two

kk'uł k'iyaggazee	nominalization	caribou leader; lit. "that whose neck is rubbed by others"
łookk'a ts'ilyaan dinh	place name	lake called "fat white fish place", 14-16 miles below the village of Huslia; Edwin Solomon's camp
kk'oon' tolidla	noun	fish eggs, roe; fish broth
kk'oontseek	noun	dried fish eggs, roe
haa	exclamation	hey!
gonaaa'	exclamation	help!

Chapter Three

nok'aghanuhlt'usk	verb	shape something by hand, knead bread
baanh yineeneełneegee	nominalization	young bear buried by its mother
doogh	adverb	around here
zo	adverb	apparently
k'itsaan'	noun	grass
dik'agheeł'eek	verb	something had gotten some now and then, repeatedly
łonh	adverb	apparently
hadnee	verb	they say
dodo	directional	little way down river, around the bend
silinh	vocative	my brother-in-law
k'oolkkoya	noun	pike
ts'eega'	noun	entrail, guts
teelzuk	verb	slurp down, without chewing
sidzeey	noun	my inner ear
hułaghudla		needle, old time needle
gheeyits	verb	broke
sik'idziyaa eehulaa ee toon' toon' toon'	(song)	song of the chikadee, translation unknown
taa'aa	noun	daddy, word used in memorial song for one's father
bits'inh	postposition	from him, it
k'ik'uh	noun	something's fat
bits'inh k'ik'uh ts'iłtłaalinh	noun phrase	who provide us with fat to chop
nigoodzagha	noun	horned owl
yoonaana	directional	way outside
loo loo loo loo		chant refrain (vocable)
di go, dee go	demonstrative	this here, this thing here
dagheelitsaa'aa, deeltsaa'aa	noun	mouse
k'akk'o yeets'in'	directional phrase	out from within something's (game animal's) pelvis
honok'ak'uhghadilidiyhł	verb	come out with something's fat repeatedly
dinh	nominalizing enclitic	place
heeyo huyo heeyo huyo		chant refrain (vocable)

Chapter Five

Totohudaatłninh	place name	lake that spills into the river (un-named lake near mouth of Kanuti River, north of Kanuti)
Ts'aatiyhdinaadakk'onh dinh	place name	Huslia; lit. "place where the forest fire burned the hill out to the river"

Index

Alatna 20-22, 56
Allakaket 12, 14, 20-22, 25, 26, 30, 35, 37, 39, 47, 50, 80, 81, 108
Attla, Catherine 66, 79
Attla, Stephen 45
Anchorage 87, 88
animal songs 77-79
Arctic City 12, 14, 20-22, 24
bear 28, 29, 75-77
Bergman, Bill 26
Bettles 20, 25, 26, 37, 38
Bidok'idniyh, Leasa & Johnny 75-77
Bifelt, Cue 92
Big Mama (Magdelen) 71, 72
Birch River 23
Black, George 80
Bremner, John 19
Burke, Mrs. 27
canoe 14, 17, 71
caribou 14, 15, 46-68
celebrations 16, 17, 74, 75
Chalatna 26, 27, 35
changes 14, 116
Charlie, Big 67, 74
Charlie, Larson 67
Charlie, Little 67, 74
chicken (grouse) 12
City of Paris 31, 32
Cleaver, Evelyn 63
crow (raven) 28-29
Cutoff 11, 14, 18, 59, 60, 112-115
dance 74, 103
death 18
Derendoff, Angeline 79
Derendoff, Richard 43, 113
disease 17, 18, 39, 40
dogs 14
Dolbaakaakk'at 17, 31
dreams 87, 88
Dubin, Sam 41-43
Dulbi 17, 19, 31, 41, 68

education 26, 27, 89-92
equal rights 105, 106
Fairbanks 87-89, 93
firefighting 85-87
fishing 24, 55-57, 66
flood 16
food 48, 49, 56, 57, 68, 71, 72
freezeup 23, 25
freighting 41, 80, 81
Galena 44, 61, 64
goldmining 22, 23, 38, 81, 82, 105
healthcare 19, 43, 110, 111
Henry, Grandma Bessie 71
Henry, Haymon 62, 63
Holy Cross 61
Hog River 41, 81-83, 105
Hog River Johnny 71, 72
Hope, Ludi 16
horses 23-25
houses (shelter) 15, 34-37, 41, 68, 73, 113
Hrdlicka, Doctor 30
Hughes 22, 41, 108
hunting 15, 23, 37, 46-51, 57, 60, 75, 76
Huntington, Jimmy 45, 83
Huntington, Sidney 44, 45, 83, 105
Huslia 11, 14, 83-86, 89-93, 112-117
hutłanee 12, 33, 76
ice 52, 53
Idler 81
Isaac, Alfred 22
Jackson, Barry 102, 103
Kallands, Edgar 39
Ketzler, Alfred 103
King, game warden 108-109
Kobuk 60
Kokrines 64
Kokrine, Rose & Peter 59-62
Koyukon language 12, 89, 118, 119
Koyukuk River 18-22, 25, 31, 32, 56, 62, 80, 81

Koyukuk Station 31, 41, 43, 44, 61, 62
land claims 102, 103
language (see Koyukon) 61, 66, 74, 75
Little William 67, 74
Lynx Creek 17
Marie, Old Man Tom 62, 63
marriage 34-36, 40, 41
medicine people 31, 39-40, 64-66
Melozi 37
missionaries 20-22, 25
muskrat hunting 35
names 20, 21
Ned & Lily 23-26
Nictune, Oscar 15
Nulato 61, 68, 103
old age 93
Old Man Bob 19
Oldman, Johnny 39
Old Man River 15-17, 23, 26, 35, 47, 56
old ways 14-17
Olin, Christine 59, 60, 64-70, 112
Parker, Henry 19, 20
Paul, Lucy & Old 23-25, 64
potlatch 17, 103
Rampart 14-16, 21
Red Shirt 17, 31
Riley, Jerry 81
Ruby 61, 64
Sackett, Jack 43, 113
Sackett, John 103
Sam, Tony 92
Sammy, Little 69, 113
school 26, 27, 89, 90, 113, 114
Simon, Andrew 26, 33
Simon, Franklin 50, 52, 86, 91, 92
Simon, Gallee (Calvin) 50, 51, 93, 94
Simon, Julia (mother) 15-18, 23-26, 33, 73

Simon, Lee 33
Simon, Lydia (Kokrine, Olin) 39, 40, 41, 52, 59-79, 87, 94
Simon, Margerite (Isaac) 34-39, 113
Simon, Michael 16
Simon, Old Man 15-18, 24-27, 30-32, 73
snow 15-17
Sommer's, Old Man 68
spring 17
St. John's of the Wilderness 20-22, 35
Steamer Nenana 17
steamboats 31, 32, 80, 81
Steven's Village 15, 102
Stickman, Joe 62-65
Stickman, Old Man 64
stores 36, 39, 41-44, 66-70, 83-85
Stuck, Archdeacon Hudson 20-22
Tanana 20, 25, 38, 39, 44, 55
Tanana Chiefs 101-103, 115
tanning 50
Teddy H 41, 42
Territory of Alaska 105, 106
trapping 27, 28, 34, 35, 39, 40, 44, 45, 69, 70, 107, 108
traveling 14-17, 37, 66-68
Vent, Bobby 44
Vent, Mary (Olin) 61, 79
Vernetti, Dominic 43, 44, 67
Vernetti, Ella 43
White, Dick 20, 21
White, Sam 71
White people 18-23, 26, 37, 38, 71, 104, 105
Wiseman 37, 38
woodsman (*nik'inla'an*) 94-101
Wright, Celia 27
Yatlin 82
young people 57, 58
Yukon River 14-16, 31, 61